The
FOCUS MODEL

The
FOCUS MODEL
Systematic School Improvement for all Schools

B. R. Jones

CORWIN
A SAGE Company

FOR INFORMATION:

Corwin
A SAGE Company
2455 Teller Road
Thousand Oaks, California 91320
(800) 233-9936
www.corwin.com

SAGE Publications Ltd.
1 Oliver's Yard
55 City Road
London EC1Y 1SP
United Kingdom

SAGE Publications India Pvt. Ltd.
B 1/I 1 Mohan Cooperative Industrial Area
Mathura Road, New Delhi 110 044
India

SAGE Publications Asia-Pacific Pte. Ltd.
3 Church Street
#10-04 Samsung Hub
Singapore 049483

Acquisitions Editor: Dan Alpert
Associate Editor: Kim Greenberg
Editorial Assistant: Cesar Reyes
Production Editor: Veronica Stapleton Hooper
Copy Editor: Janet Ford
Typesetter: C&M Digitals (P) Ltd.
Proofreader: Wendy Jo Dymond
Indexer: Karen Wiley
Cover Designer: Anupama Krishnan
Marketing Strategist: Maura Sullivan

Copyright © 2014 by Corwin

Library of Congress Cataloging-in-Publication Data

Jones, B. R. (Educator)

The Focus Model : systematic school improvement for all schools / B.R. Jones.

pages cm.
Includes bibliographical references and index.

ISBN 978-1-4833-4427-0 (pbk.)

1. School improvement programs—United States. 2. Professional learning communities—United States. 3. Effective teaching—United States. I. Title.

LB2822.82.J65 2014
371.2'07—dc23   2014008651

14 15 16 17 18 10 9 8 7 6 5 4 3 2 1

Contents

Preface

In today's turbulent world, many of our educational institutions are under fire for not producing results up to par with some of the other nations that we compete with for resources on a global level; as a result, schools face constant pressure to improve (Chenoweth, 2009). It is not that schools are allergic to change, as many researchers have stated; schools are more than willing to change. The issue is that in most cases this change does not lead schools to improved results (Elmore, 2002).

This issue is exacerbated by the fact that schools are flooded with instructional promises or "shiny baubles" that can cause educators to lose focus. In December 2012, a simple Google search for "school improvement resources" yielded 222 million results! With the volume of competing programs and practices available, is it any wonder that many schools find themselves chasing their proverbial tails—especially when the heat is on because of the "stick-and-carrot" accountability systems that are now so powerful?

Many educators feel that we need more "stick," by adding more punitive reactions against schools and districts that are not meeting goals or standards. In many cases, this myth was debunked when some districts that used the "neutron-bomb strategy" (so called because entire staffs were fired) experienced not-so-delightful results or improvements in student achievement.

Others believe that the system needs more "carrot" in the form of merit pay and other incentive programs. The problem with this strategy is that there is no research base that supports a relationship between the implementation of these types of strategies and improved student results. Is it safe to assume that we know what to do to improve schools, and for some reason, we are just not implementing these more effective practices? The question begs an answer from those who would say that the offer of more money is all we need to spur teachers and school leaders to the epiphanies that will lead to increased success.

The proposition of this book is very similar to the quote attributed to Ron Edmonds (1978):

> We can whenever, and wherever we choose, successfully teach all children whose schooling is of interest to us. We already know more than we need in order to do this. Whether we do it must finally depend on how we feel about the fact that we haven't so far.

This proposition does not mean that we are condemning all those who may not have 100 percent of their students at proficiency level or above. The idea is that we are unable to see the forest for the trees.

This book asserts that it is *not* the number of initiatives that a school or a district has in place that lead to improved results; it most definitely *is* the quality of the effective practices that the school chooses to make its focus. The bottom line is that the focus has to be on teaching and, even more, on learning. The recommendations in the chapters to come are incessantly fixated not only on student results but also, just as important, on the actions of the adults that lead to these results. It is only when we consider both factors, student results and adult actions, that we can set about the business of realizing the profound impacts on student achievement that we seek (Reeves, 2006).

My goal over the next few chapters is to reflect on the vast amount of research that is now available suggesting that we do currently have knowledge of the structures that we need in order to ensure increased student results. What invariably has led to less than desired results is how we contemplate our work and how these varied and proposed practices fit together. That is the synthesis for *The Focus Model* (TFM), taking what we discover from the latest research and using that knowledge to power up effective practices in the present.

Take some time to consider the ideas and concepts of this book. Give yourself, your district, your school, your staff, and your kids the gift of focus. I do not emphasize a plethora of initiatives in this volume. Primarily, I focus on four key components that comprise TFM. Those four components are *Learning intentions, success criteria, formative assessment,* and *professional learning communities* (PLCs). You have probably heard the axiom "The people make the difference, not the program." It is the supposition of this book and a preponderance of the research cited over the next few chapters that it is the people doing the things that have the greatest impact that make the difference— and it is that difference that translates into improved results for our students and more satisfying working conditions for our educators.

Acknowledgments

Corwin gratefully acknowledges the contributions of the following reviewers:

Elizabeth Alvarez, PhD
Principal
John C. Dore Elementary
Chicago, II

Sean Beggin
Associate Principal
Andover High School
Andover, MN

Judy Brunner
Principal
Springfield, MO

Freda Hicks
Principal
Perry Harrison School
Pittsboro, NC

About the Author

B.R. Jones is a lifelong educator working on effective school improvement with schools from the kindergarten level to universities all over the United States. B.R. started his career as a teacher and athletic coach, but over the course of 20 years in education, he has worn many hats: club sponsor, bus driver, maintenance director, building-level principal, and, for the past several years, professional learning consultant.

Most of B.R.'s experience is in schools with high minority populations and low socioeconomic conditions. When B.R. took over as the supervising principal of Wayne County High School (WCHS) in Waynesboro, Mississippi, the school faced many difficult issues; of most concern was the fact that WCHS was considered by many to be an unsafe school and a lost cause.

By leading the implementation of numerous effective practices, B.R. led WCHS to new heights in student achievement, resulting in graduates who are better prepared for college and careers, and a revamped perception by the community concerning the safety and caliber of the school.

Due to the improvements in instruction, serving at risk kids, and the increased student achievements, *U.S. News & World Report* chose WCHS as one of America's Best High Schools in 2010. In addition, B.R. was selected as the administrator of the year for the State of Mississippi in 2010. He was also named the Mississippi Educational Computing Association (MECA) administrator of the year for 2010 for the advancements in technology that he helped implement for at risk students.

B.R. completed his PhD in educational leadership at the University of Southern Mississippi in Hattiesburg, Mississippi. He also received his master's at the University of Southern Mississippi and his Bachelor of Science at the University of Mississippi.

B.R. enjoys spending time with his family and friends. He has three children and a lovely wife whom he adores.

1

The Hard Work of School Improvement

The only place success comes before work is in the dictionary.

Vincent "Vince" Lombardi

Improvement Is Tough

Certainly, we all agree that school improvement is not easy. But why is it so tough? One of the most frustrating issues is that school improvement has no ultimate destination. School improvement is a continuous journey. This dynamic is facilitated by the fact that from year to year we are constantly working with a different group of staff and students and with varying levels of resources. This often leads educators to feel exhausted by the number of dynamic variables, many of which they find are outside of their control.

The answer to this conundrum, of course, is that we must focus on the variables that are directly within our control or at the least subject to our direct influence. By focusing on our sphere of influence, we can make decisions and quantify the great impacts we are able to realize when we institute effective practices. Fundamental to this focus is the identification of a few key practices that when implemented with fidelity can have a significant impact in the two essential areas of most concern—teaching and learning.

Another reason that school improvement is tough is that many of the variables that we seek to assess in kids are really hard to measure. For example, let's identify the broad skills such as reading and problem solving as skills that are "covert" in nature. We are really not able to directly measure such skills. Instead, we rely on using inferences produced by student performance on assessments or similar tasks to make the presence of these abilities more "overt." We are unable to peel back our kids' heads and look into their brains to directly evaluate their reading or problem-solving abilities. As a result, we rely on assessments or tests to determine the functioning level of our kids at any given moment. Based on student performance on assessments, we make inferences about what they know and are able to do and to what relative degree (Popham, 2003).

The issue with this lack of direct measurement ability means that the nature of the assessments that we do use is extremely important. But even more important are the inferences that we formulate as a result of these measurements. If the measurement does not align with the expectations that we use to make inferences in relation to our kids' cognitive ability, guess what—we make an invalid inference. Now this may not sound like that big of a deal, but what if this prevents a child from graduating from high school or from obtaining entrance to a college or training program? With the types of accountability systems that many states have adopted, the stakes are very high.

We have a moral responsibility to make certain that the assessments we are using to make decisions about student knowledge and skill levels yield inferences that are reliable and valid. Are we really measuring what we intend to measure? And even more important, does this assessment allow us to make inferences about the abilities or the lack thereof of our kids? These are additional issues that cloud the picture of school improvement. Last, for teachers to make the best use of measurement data, this data should help to clarify for teachers where students are coming into the learning (i.e., are students currently at a surface or novice level of understanding, or are they at the deep or metacognitive level of understanding). Having the ability to make these in-the-moment assessments of students is at the heart of using formative assessment for planning. This type of interaction at the collegial level is at the heart of the effective professional learning community.

Finally, the plethora of activities taking place in schools must mean that we are about the business of making gains in student achievement and in staff-driven engagement in improving effectiveness, right? Not so fast. More often than not, what we find is the frantic activity of what John Kotter (2008) calls a "false sense of urgency," which is because of the pressure applied in the *carrot-and-stick* accountability systems employed in a majority of states today (p. 23). We have meetings (sometimes about meetings), we check all the boxes, we create the 500-page literacy plans, but here's the question: Does this amount of sheer activity lead to improved results? Realistically, this type of frenzied activity—the need to do it all—and do it now—usually leads to burnout and lowered morale. When it comes to school improvement, *more* is certainly not correlated with *better.* The use of fewer but more effective practices implemented deeply and successfully is how schools improve. As Lou Holtz, the famous football coach said, "A coach never lost a football game because they did not have enough plays." Schools do not fail because they do not have enough initiatives in place. They succeed by using highly impactful practices that are implemented effectively and with fidelity. In addition, how educators think about their work also has an exponential impact on the outcomes of that work. The "right" actions, and the appropriate thought processes that guide those actions, are what have proved time and again to help drive improved student results.

John Hattie (2009) speaks of this idea of focus in his book *Visible Learning* where he synthesizes more than 800 meta-analyses about the variables associated with schools that have the greatest impact on student achievement. Any system has a finite amount of resources. Whether we are talking about financial capital, physical capital, or cognitive capital, we can focus deeply on a few items at one time. The finite nature of resources reinforces the need for focusing on fewer priorities. Hattie (2012) also found that the way that people think about their work, through what he termed "mind-frames" can have a powerful effect on the impact that school leaders and teachers have within schools. According to Hattie,

> It is a set of mind frames that underpin our every action and decision in a school: it is a belief that we are evaluators, change agents, adaptive learning experts, seekers of feedback about our impact, engaged in dialogue and challenge, and developers of trust with all, and that we see opportunity in error . . . (2012, p. 159)

This important concept about how we think about our work also underpins the key driver and supports the architecture of the professional learning community (PLC) and the implementation of *The Focus Model* (TFM). DuFour, DuFour, and Eaker (2008) discuss six vital characteristics, similar to Hattie's (2012) mind-frames, which are related to the conception of how we think about our work. The six key characteristics common to all professional learning communities (PLCs) are

1. a combination of shared mission, vision, and goals all focused on student learning that drive the actions of the team.

2. a collaborative culture with the purpose of improving teaching and learning.

3. a collective look at what is working "best," and the current reality of where learning is presently for all students and adults.

4. an orientation surrounding the conception that adult action can have dramatic positive impact on student learning outcomes.

5. an orientation toward student learning outcomes as the measurement criteria of success.

6. a commitment to continuous improvement through deliberative practice and the drive to constantly measure adult impact by looking at student learning.

The goal of TFM is that we learn to focus by designing effective PLCs that are aimed at using a few high leverage practices within the confines of collaboration to solve issues related to teaching and learning. As Troen and Boles (2012) concluded, "what teachers are unable to accomplish alone, or only with great difficulty, they can accomplish more successfully in a team" (p. 7). If schools are left to focus by default, we find that they typically keep piling on one "flavor-of-the-month" initiative after another until things begin to fall off the proverbial plate. The most pressing issue arises when one of the most critical and effective research-informed strategies is one of the practices that fall by the wayside. TFM promotes a mindset of focusing on fewer research-informed practices and learning to implement those practices more effectively. As James Popham (2003) so aptly phrased, "We measure what we treasure" (p. 108). Due to our incessant grasping for the next "magic-bullet" initiative, we communicate to stakeholders that everything is a priority. In reality, what we are truly communicating is that we have no priorities. Failure is sure to be our fate when we fail to focus. This iteration of the PLC that is most concerned with monitoring educators' impact on teaching and learning is called an *Impact-Professional Learning Community (I-PLC)* and is the driver that supports TFM. Thus, the major focus of the I-PLC is the search for positive and negative evidence for the impact of instructional decisions on student and adult learning. The three central practices that are supported by the I-PLC within TFM are the development of clear learning intentions, success criteria, and the effective implementation of formative assessment practices.

It is more likely that we can and will enjoy the fruits of our labor, when we have a collaborative structure in place like the I-PLC, which is grounded in appropriate mind-frames that allow us to focus on key aspects of learning and to seek the impact of our instructional decisions. The key is to focus on a limited number of priorities supporting learning for students and adults so that we can support those priorities with effective professional development, monitoring, and follow-through. The solution is implementation of a process that creates a learning system. Have you ever started an initiative within the school with great fanfare and excitement only to have it fizzle away soon after the launch? Undoubtedly you have experienced this phenomenon in some form or fashion. It is more often than not the doomed initiative's fate because we tried to launch new programs amid the wreckage of numerous previous programs that still litter the landscape of our schools like sedimentary rock. The answer is to develop plans with limited numbers of strategies and goals so that we can muster the human, physical, and financial resources to provide them the care and nutrition required for them to grow and we can focus on building a system that is dedicated to learning. Additionally, having a structure in place, such as the I-PLC, which allows for follow-up, monitoring, and the development of individual and collective accountability for results is also critical for school improvement and the development of a systemic learning organization.

Improvement Requires Perseverance

If asked for a simple "yes" or "no" to the following questions about your school or district, how would you respond?

1. Do all educators, at all levels of the system, currently have a common conception of what it is we want all students, at all grade levels, to know and be able to do?

2. Do all educators, at all levels of the system, currently have a common conception of progress for all students on these important student-learning outcomes?

3. Do all educators, at all levels of the system, currently have effective formative assessment structures in place, at all grade levels, that allow real time instructional decisions driven by evidence of impact?

If you were able to answer yes to all three of these questions, I would first like to say, "Congratulations," because your school improvement plan is worth millions! If your answer was no to any one of the questions, then you are in good company—along with about 99.9 percent of the other schools in the United States. What that really means is that even if your school is ranked as a "high-performing" school, there remains room for improvement.

As previously mentioned, one of the most frustrating aspects of school improvement is that it is a continuous journey. This author likens it to stopping a leak in a dam holding water. When you stop the flow of water in one area, lo and behold, another spot gives way. This analogy illustrates the reason behind why having a few key strategies and goals that you can truly keep a handle on is so important. Also in order to create success, educators must be willing to maintain their focus on those effective practices. In their latest book, *Great by Choice*, Jim Collins and Morten Hansen (2011) refer to this imperative maintenance as *fanatic discipline.*

In the book, much like in another book by Collins (2001) titled *Good to Great* (2011), Collins and Hansen performed comparative analyses on companies with all major variables relatively the same but in the end took different paths when it came to success, or a lack thereof. One of the attributes of the companies that were overtly successful was the fact that they maintained focus on those few aspects that gave them the greatest results for the investment of time and resources. This reinforces the idea of focusing on what matters most. Schools invariably must maintain focus on learning. This learning is just as important for the adults as it is for the students.

Quality Over Quantity

When it comes to school improvement, there is no shortage of initiatives for sale in this day and age of mass marketing. It is no wonder that multitudes of teachers and leaders are incessantly bombarded with the next "big saving solution." In his 2009 seminal work, *Visible Learning,* what John Hattie finds even more troublesome, is that if we set the bar at zero in regard to initiatives having a positive effect size on student achievement, then pretty much everything "works." So we have multitudes of salespeople waving banners, literally, exclaiming, "Buy our product or strategy; it *works."* However, Hattie's findings reveal that the mere fact of a child just gaining 1 year of age, with the corresponding maturity that comes with that year, could have noticeable positive effects on student achievement.

Hattie (2009) makes it clear that when dealing with programs or products, we should ask more than the simple question, "Does it work?" Instead, and more significantly ask exactly how well does it work? If implemented with fidelity, what might we expect to be the positive impact on student achievement in a given year? The question then becomes not simply "What works?" but "What works best?"

The following chapters introduce four effective practices— yes, that is not a misprint, just *four* effective practices that have proved successful time and time again by multiple schools, multiple researchers, and multiple teachers and their students. These practices are the following:

1. Determining Critical Learning Intentions

2. Developing Success Criteria

3. Introducing Formative Analysis Related to Learning Intentions and Success Criteria

4. Developing Impact-Professional Learning Communities (I-PLCs), which are collaborative groups, formed to search for the effect and evidence of impact of adult actions on student learning, thus utilizing this knowledge and evidence to inform professional practice and to improve student learning.

Now, because this list is rather brief, it might lead one to the conclusion that there is nothing to school improvement. Once again, this author cautions, "Not so fast, my friend." Over the next few chapters, this book shares the effective practices that hold the power to help in any school setting (public, private, parochial, home school, and college or university) and to accelerate and improve student achievement. The only ingredient that is not included in this volume is the hard work that this process requires. The bright side is that schools, teachers, and leaders are already working very hard. Is there a way that we can refocus this work on learning in such a way to promote student growth and a renewal in teacher efficacy? There certainly is, and over the next chapters, a plan to do just that unfolds, but first a little more groundwork on a couple of important caveats before we get into the four foundational practices of TFM.

Teacher-Driven Improvement

The first point to emphasize is that school improvement has to take place in the classroom. School improvement is not something that is cooked up in some laboratory and sprinkled on faculty, staff, and kids. The people who have the most influence on student achievement within our schools, the teachers, must drive improvement. With this finding comes great responsibility on the part of teachers. Hattie (2012) asserts,

> The act of teaching requires deliberate intervention to ensure that there is cognitive change in the student; thus the key ingredients are being aware of the learning intentions, knowing when a student is successful in attaining those intentions . . . and knowing enough about the content . . . so that there is some sort of progressive development. (p. 16)

All these important aspects are inherently addressed in TFM.

Many professional development providers have gone astray by trying to "teacher-proof" school improvement strategies or programs. How can this be? Effective practices will always rule the day, not bloated three-ring binders that fit very neatly on the classroom shelf, never to be lifted again once the pitter-patter of the "spray and pray" professional development session is over.

The power of the strategies that are presented here is that they are all inherently effective because they are teacher driven. No bureaucrats needed! It is not that our political leaders are not important stakeholders, but we have to support and engage our teachers if true sustainable improvement in our schools is our goal.

People who stand before teachers and exclaim that they should be able to teach to mastery every single standard in the voluminous curriculum frameworks and have enough time to reteach and reassess as needed are not living in the same world that teachers live in on a daily basis. Normally, the people who espouse this nonsense to teachers are three or four levels removed from the classroom. It is time to wake up, America. The wheel is spinning, but the hamster is dead! Now, this author knows that to some people, what was just said could be considered tantamount to sacrilege. Hear me out; this author does not advocate eliminating standards, but does advocate taking a reasoned approach to ensure that we spend the time needed to clearly define learning intentions and success criteria so that our kids, and our educators, have the clarity needed to learn more effectively and deeply. For the sake of our kids, let's agree to make learning the constant and time the variable that we are willing to manipulate.

Classroom Performance as Measure of Success

The idea of school improvement as teacher-driven can be considered foreign in today's competitive world of new age initiatives, but the classroom should be the true measure of success. What effect can a teacher have on a child from the time that child walks into the room at the beginning of the year until the last day of the school year? This should be the measure of accountability for the effectiveness of a teacher. Any other type of measurement assumes that kids are like potted plants, with the assumptions that all the plants have the exact same requirements of sunshine, water, and temperature and that all the plants come to the nursery in the same state of health—none of them suffering from a lack of sunshine or nutrients, but all at the exact same level of fitness. You know, come to think of it, this line of thinking does not even hold for potted plants. Why in the world would we expect it to work for kids? But this is exactly the type of accountability system that the majority of states have implemented over the past few years.

This author hopes to shed some light on how to make this type of accountability more visible so that we can support the hard work of teachers within classrooms to help all kids achieve the intended learning outcomes at the proficient level regardless of the type of standard or the grade level. But before this author talks about the four core effective practices of TFM, just a few more insights on the ideas of focus, effective monitoring, and efficacy.

KEY CONSIDERATIONS

It is not the number of initiatives that a school has in place that ultimately leads to success or failure. Invariably, it is the quality of the few initiatives with deep implementation that has the greatest potential for positive effect on teaching and learning. In addition, the way that educators think about the work also has a great impact on the outcomes of their work. School improvement is not a spectator sport. It takes effective practices deeply implemented by all involved. With positive results comes the opportunity to make the cultural changes that are needed to foster sustainability of improvement efforts. We all have a part to play.

Guiding Questions

1. If you survey all the faculty and staff in your school or district, how many initiatives are perceived to be in place at this time?

2. Do all stakeholders know your current priorities? Are some of the initiatives identified by staff no longer considered "in place"?

3. Can you directly link these initiatives to quantifiable improvements in student results? Does this level of improvement justify the investment of time, personnel, and money?

4. How do you currently measure the success of initiatives in relation to student results?

5. How do you measure implementation? Are you truly implementing these initiatives with fidelity?

6. Are all teachers clear about what students should learn from grade to grade?

7. Are all teachers clear about what it means to be proficient on these important student-learning outcomes? Do teachers have a common conception of progress? What about students?

8. What structures are in place that ensure educators in your school or district know the impact of their professional practice on student-learning outcomes?

2

The Keys

Focus, Monitoring, Efficacy, and Continuous Learning

One reason so few of us achieve what we truly want is that we never direct our focus; we never concentrate our power. Most people dabble their way through life, never deciding to master anything in particular.

Tony Robbins

The Gift of Focus

When we survey the educational landscape, 46 states plus the District of Columbia are in the midst of implementing more rigorous academic content standards in the form of the Common Core State Standards (2010). The four states of Texas, Virginia, Alaska, and Nebraska, are implementing more rigorous standards of their own development. In addition there is a major initiative to revamp vocational education in many states with the Career Pathways Initiative (Mississippi State, 2012). This is a joint initiative of K–12 education, community colleges, and the industry that requires a good amount of time and effort on the part of teachers, students, and support staff to plan and implement effectively.

If this were not enough, a majority of states also have to implement new teacher and administrative evaluation programs in response to applications by the states for federal competitive grant funds through a 5-year program called "Race to the Top." For states going after a share of the $4.35 billion dollars available, the application also required the arduous task of revamping their evaluation systems. Additionally, another federal initiative, the reauthorization of the Elementary and Secondary Education Act in 1965, provided states the opportunity to apply for waivers from the deepening sanctions brought about by the increasing targets related to the 2001 No Child Left Behind Act (Popham, 2013).

These elements have led to what some educators refer to as *the perfect storm*. Many educators have been supplied just enough information about each of these major undertakings to become bewildered and anxious. Those states and districts that attempted to be proactive with so many initiatives mandated at once are still feeling overwhelmed. What is a well-intentioned educator to do? The answer is that whether at the classroom level, building level, or district level, it is essential to focus on what matters most—the learning.

The way to weather this storm is improved student results despite more rigorous standards and other drains on time and resources. The way to ensure success is to focus on deep implementation of the four-part *Focus Model* (TFM; see Figure 2.1).

Even if a school or district has been successful in the past, with the new standards and other mandates facing it, there is no guarantee that past actions will continue to produce positive results. TFM houses the four essential effective practices that any standards-based organization can use to implement standards with fidelity and provide the support in the form of monitoring and efficacy building that success requires. The remainder of this book is devoted to discussing each level of TFM in detail; it serves as a guide for any institution seeking to be successful in the process of school improvement and standards implementation with a focus on learning for the students and system adults.

Standards

Standards represent the fairest and most equitable way to measure performance and must be the objective focus of school improvement. In a norm-based system, assessment is about comparing one student against another to determine relative achievement. This sets up a situation where we must have winners and losers. James Popham

Figure 2.1   The Focus Model

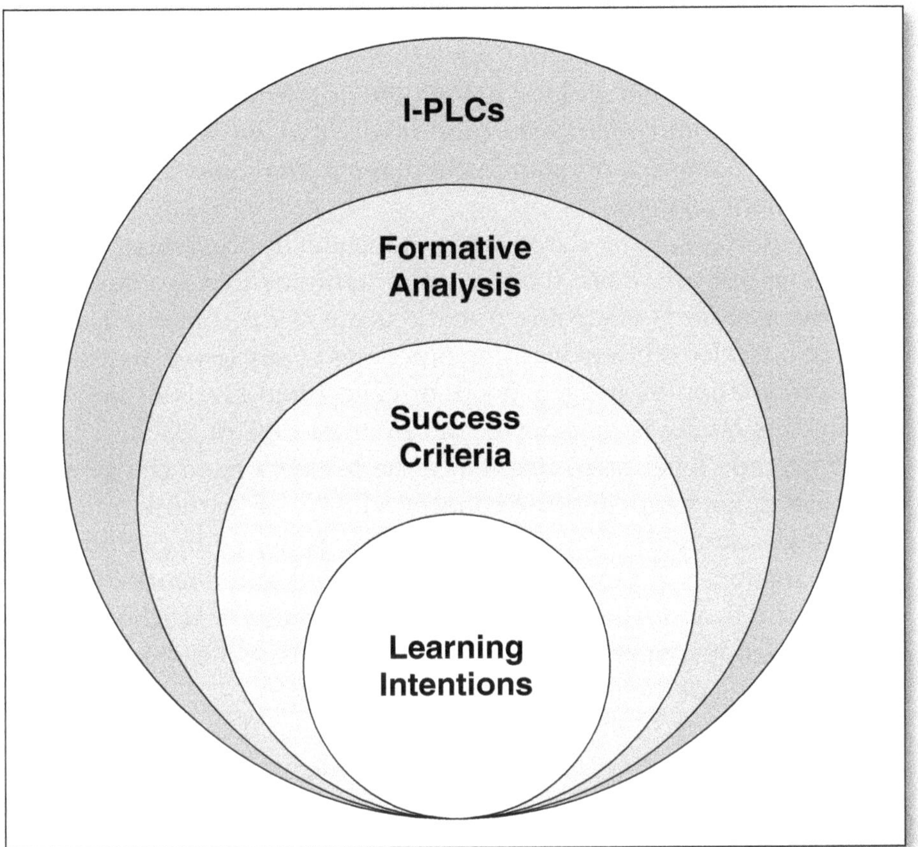

(2003) describes this as one of the issues with using norm-referenced testing inappropriately to measure learning and teacher effectiveness. Effective norm-referenced tests must have a spread in scores, and to achieve this score spread, these tests rely on test items of dubious character. If too many students answer a question correctly, test developers toss that question because it does not facilitate the spread needed to make norm-based comparisons. Now think about that for a moment. Because of the nature of norm-referenced testing, if our teachers do a bang-up job teaching a particular standard to the point that a majority of our kids correctly answer the questions related to that learning intention, we have to toss that question.

This is a mind-boggling practice, especially considering that we are supposed to operate in a standards-based environment. In a standards-based system, all students should have an opportunity to reach the rigorous bar of the clearly articulated standard. That is, if students can demonstrate the knowledge, skill, and affect required of the standard, they deserve to be considered proficient on that standard. But we do love our winners and losers. This author is all for competition in athletics, band, and the numerous other wonderful programs we have within our schools. However, can we agree that when it comes to all kids having the opportunity to learn math, language arts, and science to high levels that we should toss the bell curve? Focusing on standards plays a vital role in the school improvement process.

As important as standards are in the school improvement process, even more important are the learning intentions that are developed from the standards. Learning intentions are defined as the learning goals or intended student learning outcomes of any lesson that should be a combination of surface, deep, or conceptual levels of knowing. Ideally, this clarity is first developed by the I-PLC of teachers teaching that grade level or course. Once the teachers have clarity about the surface, the deep, and the conceptual level of learning outcomes expected of students, then the teachers are better equipped to share these intentions with their students. According to the work of Gayle, Preiss, Burrell, and Allen (2006), "Clarity is defined as teachers ability to unambiguously explain ideas and directions and discern student understanding of the material presented" (p. 268).

When looking at effects on student learning, Hattie (2009, 2012) and Hattie and Yates (2014) found that "teacher clarity" (Hattie, 2009, p. 125) ranks number nine of the 150 top influences on student achievement. The collaborative clarity that comes from I-PLCs working across grades and courses to identify critical learning intentions is a valuable first step in implementing a model of school improvement that powers this concept of *teacher clarity* across classrooms, schools, and systems.

Monitoring

One of the key results of developing clarity of intended outcomes is the enhanced ability to clearly identify present relationship in regard to goals and the intended target. The I-PLC process begins with the search and identification of key data and then the formulation of long-term (1–3 years), mid-term (6–12 months), and short-term (1–6 weeks) goals. These goals are built around success points in relation to a limited number of areas of prioritized improvement. This process is most powerful when it occurs at the classroom level. This grassroots level of involvement leads to more effective monitoring and also helps those involved in the work to more readily "own" the solutions. One of the issues with succumbing to the mind-numbing practice of showering staff with "flavor-of-the-month" initiatives is that these programs are impossible to monitor due to the volume. The key to effective monitoring is this data search and the goal setting at the forefront of the focus model's process. According to Thomas Guskey (2014), "Although data are essential to making apt decisions, the quality and appropriateness of particular data depend on their accuracy and relevance in answering specific questions in a particular context" (p. 2). In TFM, the belief is that the initial dive into the data helps to clarify which questions need to be asked, and also which goals need to be set and sought. As Guskey states, "After deciding the specific desired goals with regard to student learning, decisions about the most appropriate means will be much easier to make" (2014, p. 8). In addition, this initial data review helps us to hone the number of learning intentions to focus on during instruction, assessment, and planning. The more narrow the focus, the more we can strategically use the available resources to meet the challenges of reaching our intended goals.

Even the most well-behaved students, when left unattended for too long, eventually create mischief for themselves. The same issue holds true for the most powerful strategies or initiatives if we do not monitor their effectiveness and give feedback about the results. It is not just the act of monitoring, such as checking a box on a checklist; it is much more the rich dialogue and the opportunity for effective feedback and reflection that makes monitoring so powerful. If we implement change within our schools, yet make no provision for this type of two-way feedback loop to ensure proper implementation, then we truly do a disservice to everyone involved in the process.

The nonverbal cue of a lack of follow-through is very powerful. An example at the classroom level is when a teacher states a behavioral expectation and then does not follow through with consequences when a student chooses not to meet this expectation. Similarly, an example at the building level plays out when a new initiative is placed on teachers' plates, such as a strategy to implement nonfiction writing across content areas, but then the administrator never again asks to see evidence of the effects of the strategy on student results. This type of scenario plays out at the district level as well. In some cases, we are accustomed to this type of behavior in schools, because new initiatives seem to come and go, just like the changing of the days. Many times, the culprit is our failure to articulate just how we can monitor the issue before we ever start implementation. Thus, our plans are doomed to fail, because they forget to incorporate the paramount detail of a built-in monitoring system within the proposed change.

Even more important, we usually fail to identify those initiatives that have long outlived their usefulness before we ever start a new one, and, in most cases, we do not communicate this information throughout the system. Isn't it odd that we fill calendar after calendar, year after year, with the initiatives that we are going to implement, but after having spent more than 20 years in schools, this author cannot recall a specific discussion of initiatives that we were specifically going to stop executing? If we are truly going to monitor the initiatives we implement with the feedback, deliberate practice, and reflection that defines effective monitoring, then two things must happen. Number one, we must limit the number of initiatives, and number two, we must be willing to openly and honestly eliminate those practices that are not having a positive impact on student results. We must be willing to create and communicate the list of activities we intend to stop doing.

Any school improvement effort is only as good as the embedded monitoring structure. The power of TFM comes from the I-PLC process that is embedded at the district, school, and classroom levels that help ensure an alignment of goals, strategies, and intended outcomes. As the name makes clear, *Impact-PLCs* are charged with the constant search for evidence, both positive and negative, of the impact that our strategies and interventions are having for students and adults learning, and most importantly, using this evidence in an ongoing systematic way to improve results for students and the professional educators.

Efficacy

The *Merriam-Webster Online Dictionary* (2012a) defines the term *efficacy* as "the power to produce an effect." School improvement requires efficacy at multiple levels (See Figure 2.2). There is the self-efficacy of the person who initiates the change or at least advocates for the change. Change builds momentum when a number of like-minded individuals come together to form a guiding coalition. Not that a school should wait until they get 100 percent buy-in before the process begins, but it does require efficacy on the part of the person introducing the change. This may manifest itself simply as the belief that as an individual, one can have a positive impact on that school. Taking a page from Barber, Moffit, and Kihn's (2011) work in *Deliverology*, the I-PLC can be compared to a "guiding coalition" (pp. 35–36). Barber and colleagues define a guiding coalition as, "the group of people that enables the pursuit of your system's aspirations" (2011, p. 35). These authors may be stretching this concept by their comparison to the concept of a group of influential persons that could be considered the "Tipping Point," as made famous by Malcolm Gladwell. According to Gladwell (2006, p. 9), "The tipping point is that magic moment when an idea, trend, or social behavior crosses a threshold, tips, and spreads like wildfire." In this book, the efficacy tipping points we hope to provoke and incite are related to the previously noted mind-frames of John Hattie (2012) and identified as essential requirements for systemic school change.

Once positive results are experienced by others in the school, the snowball effect begins to actually change the culture of the school. Jim Collins (2001) refers to this as the *Fly Wheel Effect*. As momentum and success build, improvement gets to a point where it almost becomes self-sustaining. This facilitates the development of collective efficacy at the school level. This is a powerful force in the sustainability of any change.

Last, at the district level, for the resources to be allocated and support provided to institute a change of any magnitude, collective efficacy—or, at a minimum, self-efficacy of a person of influence—is important. For long-term sustainability, district-level efficacy is critical. Many excellent initiatives at the school level soon wither away without support from the district. Efficacy is vitally important at all levels when discussing school improvement. John Hattie (2012) made the following assertion after looking at a preponderance of the evidence for the impact of efficacy, "the differences between high-effect and low-effect teachers are primarily related to the attitudes and expectations that teachers have when they decide on the key issues of teaching . . ." (p. 23). This speaks to the power of efficacy and the importance of engaging teachers directly in any process for school improvement.

The real-time results provided by TFM facilitate the development and the maintenance of efficacy as the essential elements of celebrating success, effective monitoring, and focus are embedded in each step.

Improving Professional Practice

In addition to improvements in student results, another result of effective implementation of *The Focus Model* should ideally be improved professional practice for educators. When examining the 2011 *Standards for Professional Development* (formerly the National Council for Staff Development), each one is aptly represented in TFM.

Figure 2.2   Levels of Efficacy

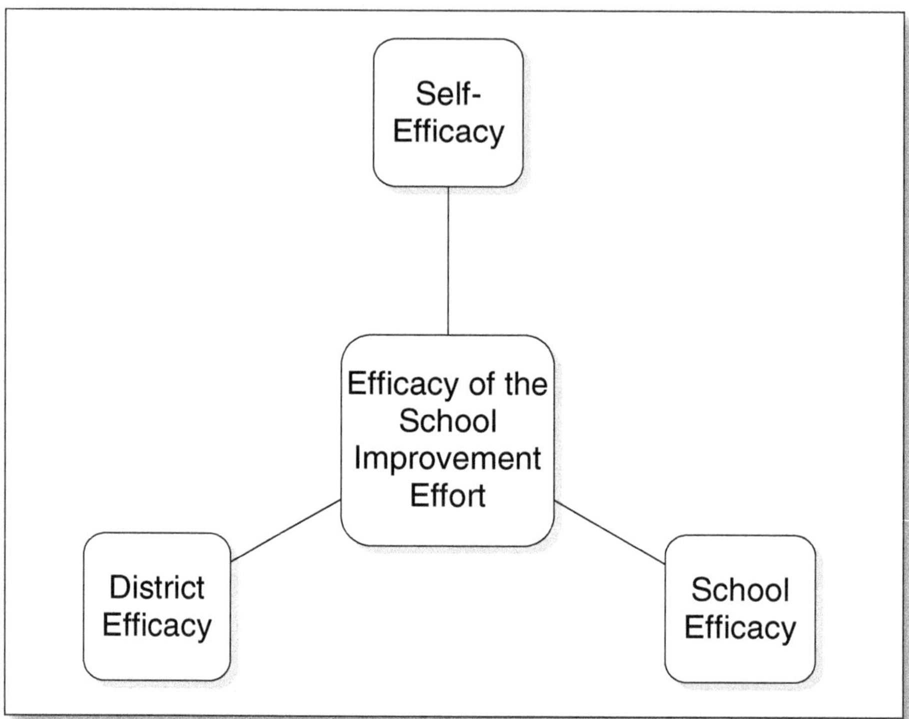

Each of the italicized phrases corresponds to one from the list of Learning Forward Standards for Professional Learning. Standard 1 speaks to *Learning Communities* as goal oriented, results driven, and committed to continuous improvement of professional practice and student results (Learning Forward, 2013). The I-PLC structure embedded within TFM attends to the commitment of collegial learning and the development of collaborative problem solving in a similar manner as a traditional PLC. However, there is one major distinction: Some PLCs are prone to get off mission and to morph into glamorized gab sessions. In contrast, the I-PLC is about focusing on the impact that we have on student learning outcomes and the impact that our collective work has on our professional practice, specifically translating to improvements in the classroom. Thus at the heart of TFM is the attention to creating a true community of educators seeking to collaborate around the issues related to effective teaching and positive impacts on student learning at all knowledge levels (surface, deep, and conceptual).

Standard 2 addresses the role of *Leadership*. In TFM, leadership support, interaction, feedback, and monitoring are essential. In the purest sense, instructional leadership is vital in the support and development of TFM within a school or system. Regarding student achievement, Viviane Robinson (2011) found five essential leadership dimensions that have the highest effect size for school leaders. The dimensions are "establishing goals and expectations, resourcing strategically, ensuring quality teaching, leading teacher learning and development, and ensuring a safe and orderly environment" (Robinson, 2011, p. 9). The greatest effect size for leadership was related to the dimension of *leading teacher learning and development (*d = *0.84).* What Robinson found was that "the more leaders focus their relationships, their work, and their learning on the core business of teaching and learning, the greater will be their influence on student outcomes" (2011, p. 15). This is certainly the goal of TFM. In addition to looking at the impact of instructional strategies on student learning outcomes, leaders should measure the impact of their leadership strategies on the outcomes of effective collaboration leading to tangible products. For instance, learning intentions, success criteria, and aligned formative assessment instruments used to gather data to make real-time decisions and to make ongoing adjustments to professional practice. Other key data points could be related to seeing new or different strategies used in classrooms that are directly aligned to helping extend the learning of already proficient students or that help with filling in the gaps for students not presently proficient.

Standard 3 speaks to effectively utilizing *Resources.* In TFM, we strive to tap into the greatest resource available in schools that is the resource of highly effective, inspired, and passionate teachers. When teachers share best practice, look at problems from different perspectives, and are willing to have conversations about the facts regarding the impact that we are having on students, then they do not get bogged down in the isolationist culture that fosters the moniker "You leave me alone and let me teach, and I will do the same for you," and we begin to develop better solutions to the hard work of learning. Strategic resourcing is also an important leadership dimension discovered to have a significant impact on student learning in Viviane Robinson's (2011) research. When leaders utilize the financial, personnel, and other resources strategically in a manner that supports the improvement of teaching and learning, we can expect higher effects on student learning outcomes. The goal of TFM is that due to the clarity of focus (learning intentions), the common conception of progress (success criteria), and the knowledge of where students are in relation to the intended learning outcomes (formative assessment), teachers make better informed decisions apropos of effective teaching and learning.

Standard 4 of the *Learning Forward 2011 Standards for Professional Learning* speaks to the effective use of *Data.* This is a critical standard, as many times schools are inundated with collecting data for the sake of compliance, but the disheartening aspect of this enterprise is that many times much of this data does not lead to substantial, if any, improvements in professional prowess or student-learning outcomes. In this aspect, TFM is in line with the thoughts of Thomas Guskey (2014) when he wrote, "Since our primary goal in professional learning is to improve results for all students, the most important level of data to consider is that closest to students: the classroom level" (p. 15). That is the primary data source that the I-PLCs utilize to monitor short-term and mid-term goals, and utilizing more longitudinal types of data to monitor progress toward longer term goals of improvement.

Standard 5 relates to the concept of *Learning Designs*. In TFM, since I-PLCs are primarily concerned with illuminating and making visible the impact that educators are having on student learning outcomes, then understanding learning theory, particularly how students learn is critical. The ability to recognize where students are in relation to learning at each level (surface, deep, and conceptual) is critical to knowing where students are in relation to learning intentions and where teachers and students need to go next to meet the success criteria. According to the latest work of John Hattie (2014), "Expert teachers' understanding of students is such that they are more able to provide developmentally appropriate learning tasks that engage, challenge, and even intrigue students without boring or overwhelming them—they know 'where to next.'" (p. 107). This speaks to the need of effective teachers to be able to diagnose where students are in relation to the learning intentions, and to know what feedback students might need to either extend learning if students are already proficient or intervene when students might need help filling in the gaps (Hattie, 2012).

Standard 6 refers to the constant battle that schools face when it comes to *Implementation*. The *Merriam-Webster Online Dictionary* (2013b) defines *fidelity* as "the quality or state of being faithful; accuracy in details: exactness." How many times have you been involved with the implementation of an initiative that promised improved results only to be disappointed as those results somehow eluded you? On the contrary, have you been part of an implementation of an initiative that did deliver and meet expectations? As you consider these two opposites, what were the underlying differences that ultimately lead to the dissimilar results? Odds are that the difference was the fidelity of implementation. In TFM, within the I-PLC process, implementation is monitored in at least two of the seven steps of the process (see Figure 2.3).

The last two steps of the process identified as critical to student success are directly related to evaluating implementation of the proposed plans to attack student-learning deficits on the identified learning

Figure 2.3   I-PLC Seven-Step Process

Adapted from the Iowa Professional Development Model Framework (2009); Irwin and Farr (2004); Birenbaum, Kimron, Shilton, and Shahaf-Barzilay (2010); and by Killion (2013).

intentions. In Step 6, I-PLCs determine if the strategies or interventions selected in Step 4 produced the intended results from the impact evidence gathered from the testing of the hypotheses (implementation of the intended strategies). The first consideration is to ask, "Did we implement the interventions as we had intended and what evidence do we have to support this fidelity of implementation?" The same type of question can be asked about leadership or support strategies and interventions that were introduced seeking improved impact at the classroom-level I-PLC and at the building-level I-PLC. As a complement to the classroom-level and building-level I-PLCs, similar types of questions surrounding the development of effective PLC culture, training, and follow-up and monitoring can be asked at the system level. So as you can see, within TFM, each level of the system, district/ provincial level, building level, and classroom level, is concerned with discovering not only the impact on student learning outcomes, but also on implementation of the adult leadership and instructional strategies as well (see Figure 2.4).

The key to recognizing the power of implementation is recognizing the power that we as educators have with respect to the process of learning. What multiple authors and educators—Hattie (2009, 2012); Hattie and Yates (2014); Robinson (2011); Popham (2003, 2008); Troen and Boles (2012); DuFour, DuFour, and Eaker (2008); and DuFour, DuFour, Eaker, and Karhanek (2010)—all found is that when educators deeply and effectively implement the practices of TFM with fidelity, schools can have profound positive impacts on student-learning outcomes.

The final standard in the *Learning Forward 2011 Standards for Professional Learning* is related to the conception of *Outcomes*. The total sum of the activity of TFM is the search for evidence related to the educators' impact at all levels of the system on the following: the outcomes of improved professional practice, and the impact on student learning results as measured by multiple agreed on indices related ultimately to essential student learning outcomes. This hand-in-glove fit of TFM intentions with the Learning Forward recommendations of the standards for professional development) combined with the

Figure 2.4   Relationship of Implementation to Impact

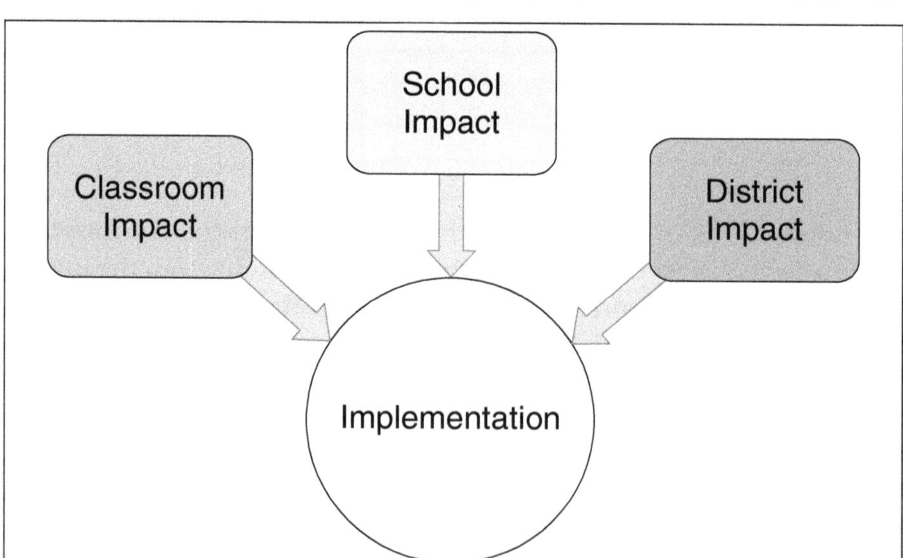

support of some of the most well respected researchers and practitioners in the field of education speak to the potential that can be found within TFM when the various components are implemented effectively, and when the outcomes are measured in indices related to professional practice and student learning outcomes. The key is the effective implementation of the I-PLC process with the primary responsibility of searching out the impact that all educators are having on student learning and, in turn, professional growth and collegial learning. These are two outcomes that we can all agree should be the focus of any professional and school-improvement strategy.

KEY CONSIDERATIONS

The key considerations for any school improvement effort are focus, monitoring, efficacy, and continuous professional learning and growth. Without attention to these four key elements, school improvement likely fails. TFM attends to all four of these key elements within each foundational piece. The key to the success of this model is efficacy being built at all levels of the system based on improved results and the learning that takes place not only at the students' level, but at the educators' level as well. Success breeds success!

Guiding Questions

1. How does the idea of focusing on fewer initiatives make sense?

2. Is monitoring currently embedded in the initiatives that are in place within your school or district? Is this monitoring ultimately measured in student results?

3. How can focusing on fewer initiatives and going deeper with implementation help build confidence in those involved in the improvement process?

4. Have you seen a lack of efficacy defeat initiatives of school improvement?

5. What are some of the ways you are prepared to share the improved results that become a reality with the deep implementation of TFM?

6. What structures are currently in place that support professional growth in the search for increased student results?

7. How do you and your colleagues presently seek to know the impact you have on students? How can this investigation be improved?

3

From Standards to Learning Intentions

Our goals can only be reached through a vehicle of a plan, in which we must fervently believe, and upon which we must vigorously act. There is no other route to success.

Pablo Picasso

What Do We Want All Students to Learn?

One of the most fundamental questions guiding the work of the professional learning community is, "What do we hold essential for all students to know and be able to do to be prepared for college and careers?" In two words, the answer to this question within TFM—learning intentions. Learning intentions are the curricular ends that we hope students reach after effective instruction. The problem with the standards movement is that because of the broad nature of many academic content standards, there are many implied learning intentions contained within a single content standard. It is only when educators are attentive to clearly identifying these embedded curricular aims before instruction takes place that we can hope to successfully and clearly articulate exactly what is essential for all students to know and be able to do. This examination of the standards provides the clarity needed for educators to not only identify the learning intentions of the content standards, but also to create a common conception of what it means for students to successfully master the learning intentions. This concept of success is referred to as success criteria in TFM; we discuss success criteria in more detail in Chapter 4.

Domains of Learning

When discussing the knowledge, skills, and dispositions we hope students learn, we can examine learning in three particular domains: *cognitive, affective, and psychomotor* (Oliva, 2009; Popham, 2008). By far the most common domain that receives the lion share of attention within schools is the *cognitive* dimension where learning outcomes are located. Cognitive learning outcomes relate to knowledge, principles, dates, facts, vocabulary, and concepts that are considered declarative knowledge that students need to learn. In addition to the declarative cognitive knowledge, educators also add to this domain the requisite intellectual skills necessary for this stage, such as steps in problem solving, effective writing, algorithms, and the like. These types of learning outcomes are usually included in high-stakes assessments; thus, they lend themselves to creating a sense of urgency and a need for a greater degree of attention, especially in this era of increased accountability in relation to students' progress (Popham, 2008).

Though, in many cases, they don't receive as much attention on assessments that decide high-stakes accountability, learning outcomes of the *affective* persuasion are also important to consider. These affective student outcomes describe the values, interests, and attitudes we hope students acquire as a result of their involvement in formal education. Recognizing the importance of cognitive outcomes does not diminish how worthwhile it is that students foster an attitude that values the challenge of learning. In addition to learning math facts and procedural skills, it is also meaningful for students to develop a heightened interest in problem solving by using mathematics as a means to an end. Additionally, if students develop a lifelong love for reading as a result of the experiences they had in their language arts classroom, this by-product is considered by many one of the most important outcomes of education.

Last, learning outcomes are also housed in the *psychomotor* domain. The *Merriam-Webster* (2014b) dictionary defines *psychomotor* as "of or relating to motor action directly proceeding from mental activity." Thus, this domain relates to learning associated with students' small and large muscle groups. These types of activities might be displayed in the form of dance, keyboarding, or shooting a basketball. Again, anyone who has had the pleasure to see the beauty and grace of a ballet performance would certainly agree that this domain is also a valuable learning ambition.

The Need for Limiting the Number of Curricular Aims

One of the greatest obstacles facing well-meant educators is the overabundance of intended learning outcomes they are expected to teach. Multiple researchers (Ainsworth, 2003a; Marzano, 2003; Popham, 2003; Schmoker, 2011) recognize the need to identify a prioritized list of standards and or learning outcomes that make the process of deep learning and assessment possible.

The problem with many of the standards documents is that they are so voluminous that there is never enough instructional time to teach, assess, reteach, and reassess as required to achieve student success. All too often this constraint leads teachers to pick the learning outcomes they choose to pursue based on their individual judgments. In turn, this creates fragmentation in what is taught from classroom to classroom, because teachers vary in which standards they deem as more important than others. This type of isolationism can lead to inequity when it comes to students having the "opportunity to learn" essential knowledge and skills (Marzano, 2003, p. 18).

Robert Marzano (2003) coined the term "Guaranteed and Viable Curriculum" to describe that the *opportunity to learn* and *time* were the foundational pieces of the number one school-level factor impacting student achievement (p. 22). The power of this factor is illuminated when teachers clearly articulate precisely what students need to know and be able to do (guaranteed curriculum) and structure and prioritize this curriculum in such a way that it is viable (i.e., meaning that there is the time available to teach, assess, and reteach, and reassess the curriculum as necessary for learning). Of the 11 factors identified by Marzano's meta-analyses of more than 35 years of educational research, this factor was ranked the highest in impact on student achievement. Marzano reasoned that if students are not taught the content or given the opportunity to learn it and if they are not given sufficient time to interact with the content to gain a deeper understanding of it, then odds are that the students will not learn it.

In this study, Marzano (2003) also estimated that in a survey of all the standards that students are accountable for learning from kindergarten to Grade 12, a reasonable estimation is that it would take 15,465 hours for the average student to learn this knowledge and skill to mastery. Taking this a step further, Marzano then estimated that there are only roughly 9,042 hours of instructional time available to students in their journey from kindergarten to Grade 12. Given that information, then to teach, assess, reteach, and reassess students as recommended by the teachers in this study looking at the typical content expected of kids in grade school, Marzano found that schools only have two options: either eliminate some of the content to be taught or extend schooling from "K–12 to K–22" (2003, pp. 24–25).

It is not so much a question of whether the content can be "covered," as much as it is whether the content can actually be taught. James Popham perceives the issue of having so many standards as a very serious problem that must be addressed if teachers are to hope to do an adequate job of teaching. As he relates in his book *Test Better, Teach Better (Popham, 2003),* if attempts are not made to narrow the focus of instructional planning, this creates the impossible task of being able to deeply assess an endless number of standards with fidelity. Popham (2003) goes on to state that "measurement of innumerable content standards is impossible. It is definitely possible to assess a more limited number of high-priority content standards" (p. 35).

In his book *Focus,* Mike Schmoker (2011) agrees and speaks to the need to reduce the number of content standards or learning outcomes that make up the bulk of instructional focus "by about 50 percent—even more for language arts" (p. 43).

Identifying Desirable Outcomes

In order to select the most desirable learning outcomes, we need a common system, and this is most readily done with collaborative groups of teachers teaching the same course or grade-level content. Completing this process collaboratively is highly desirable compared to having teachers complete it individually room by room. Again reinforcing the quest of ensuring equity and fairness from classroom to classroom for all students. The goal is to objectively identify the most essential learning outcomes to serve as the basis for the most essential learning intentions so that the school can more readily define the critical knowledge, skills, and dispositions that all students need to be successful and, most important, have the time needed to teach it well.

James Popham (2008) recommends three key filters for use in selecting potentially important learning outcomes. These three filters to determine if a student-learning outcome is worthwhile are *significance, teachability,* and *testability.*

When speaking of significance, the element under scrutiny relates to "Is this curricular aim truly important for student success in the future?" In this age of the implementation of more rigorous standards, we certainly are discussing the concept of producing college and career ready secondary students. In the case of Pre-K students, these learning outcomes are related to preparation for kindergarten. Once teachers determine that the particular curricular aim is significant for students to learn, educators move on to consider the other two filters.

The *Merriam-Webster* (2014c) defines *teach* as "to cause or help (someone) to learn about a subject by giving lessons." *Ability* refers to "competence in doing" (Merriam-Webster, 2014a).

Teachability then is a filter that refers to a teacher's efficacy to adequately teach the intended curricular aim. The difference in significance and teachability is that it may be a source of growth for teachers if they identify key curricular targets which they may not currently feel they have the level of expertise to adequately teach. When looking at the Common Core State Standards (CCSS; 2010) that have been adopted by a majority of states in the United States, there is a clear expectation by teachers across the schools that literacy is a shared obligation. According to the standards document for English Language Arts (ELA), "The Standards insist that instruction in reading, writing, speaking, listening, and language be a shared responsibility within the school" (CCSS, 2010, p. 4). Teachers in these areas may feel that teaching writing might be outside of the realm of their expertise. With explicit expectations like those articulated in the Common Core Standards, the teachability of certain standards might not be one of choice, but of necessity. As a result, a teacher certainly might feel compelled to include such curricular outcomes on the important list.

Curricular outcomes are truly not operationalized until we measure them. On the eve of the first official assessments related to the Common Core Standards, this reality is causing angst among American teachers. Testability of a curricular aim is an important consideration as to whether it is chosen as worthwhile for teachers and students to pursue. If the curricular aim is not measureable, how can teachers determine if it is met? Take the example of the statement "understand the writing process." How do we measure a student's *understanding?* However, we can certainly measure the student-learning outcome, for example by asking the student to "create an expository essay on the workings of the internal combustion engine." This curricular aim lends itself more readily to measurement than the previous example that seeks a quantification or qualification of the term *understanding.*

The key conception here is that we need a process for answering one of the most fundamental questions that a professional learning community asks of its members: "What knowledge, skill, and dispositions do we expect all of our kids to master?" This question is fundamental to the work of the I-PLC in TFM, because we begin the articulation of the answer to this important question with our model—the identification of the learning outcomes, synonymous with curricular aims or content standards, with the primary focus of our instructional efforts determined by asking if the aim is significant, teachable, and testable.

Surface Versus Deep Thinking

In the identification of learning intentions derived from the targeted curricular aims, it is important to make the distinction between two key levels of thinking. Most key systems for classifying the depth of thinking or knowledge of students have a demarcation between the concepts of surface-level and deeper level thinking. In Bloom's (2001) Revised Taxonomy, the levels of thinking from least complex to more complex are as follows:

- Remembering,
- Understanding,
- Applying,
- Analyzing,
- Evaluating, and
- Creating.

In Norman Webb's (1997a) Depth of Knowledge schema, the depth of knowledge (DOK) also ranges from the lowest levels to the higher levels as follows:

- DOK 1—Recall and Remember,
- DOK 2—Skills and Concepts,
- DOK 3—Strategic Thinking and Reasoning, and
- DOK 4—Extended Thinking.

Looking at the two different schema, one can see in Bloom's that going from the first three levels of thinking to the last three there is an increase in the depth of processing. In Webb's DOK, it is widely recognized that as we move beyond DOK 1, we begin to expect more rigorous thinking from students. In both cases, it can be conceptualized that we are moving from a surface to a deeper level of thinking in terms of learning expectations and outcomes for student performance. Knowing where the intentions fall on this continuum can help teachers gauge where students enter learning, and also can be beneficial in helping to inform current and future instructional decisions based on this knowledge. Therefore, as the intentions are being developed, this makes the process of determining the level of thinking required by learning intentions a worthwhile exercise.

Declarative Versus Procedural Knowledge

Another consideration in the development of learning intentions is the particular type of knowledge. The two basic types of knowledge are *declarative* and *procedural.* Declarative knowledge is related to facts, dates, concepts, and principles. Procedural knowledge is related to skills, algorithms, and processes (Nuthall, 2000). During the implementation of instruction, the importance of identifying the type of knowledge has instructional implications based on the type of guided and independent practice that teachers subscribe for students. For declarative knowledge, research reveals that four to six exposures with no more than 2 days between exposures was successful in helping students attain at least 80 percent proficiency in related assessments of this knowledge. Procedural knowledge requires students to have between 20 and 24 deliberate practices with the skill to reach a threshold of 80 percent proficiency. Initially, massed practice when students are first learning the skill was more effective followed by intermittent practice afterward in order to help fight against the extinction of the skill (Nuthall, 2000).

Learning Intentions

Once the broad curricular aims or content standards are narrowed to a more manageable number, or at least placed in a rank order of priority, we then must determine the progression of enabling knowledge and skill that students must master to be considered proficient on the targeted curricular aim. In the case of the Common Core Standards, it is understood that the standards themselves represent the end of year expectation for student performance. In the Common Core Standards for English Language Arts (2010) document, we find the following confirmation of this important caveat. The document states, "The K–12 grade-specific standards define end-of-year expectations and a cumulative progression designed to enable students to meet college and career readiness expectations no later than the end of high school" (p. 4).

The term learning intentions as used herein this book is synonymous with what many classify as learning progressions. Popham (2008) defines a learning progression as "a sequenced set of subskills or bodies of enabling knowledge that it is believed students must master en route to mastering a more remote curricular aim" (p. 24). What learning intentions truly represent, then, is a teachers' best hypothesis in regard to the chunks of knowledge, both declarative and procedural, that students need to master on the journey of learning toward mastery of the broader standard. Merriam-Webster (2014c) defines *hypothesis* as "an interpretation of a practical situation or condition taken as a ground for action." This is an important point because at its core a teacher's hypothesis is an educated guess based on the content knowledge and experience of the teacher. It is unlikely that all students will advance in a linear fashion in lockstep through the learning progression. Some students might skip one of more learning intentions to the finish line, and other students might not have the prerequisite skills to tackle even the earliest surface-level intentions in the plan. This is why it is critical that teachers are attentive to how students are progressing within the learning and also at what levels, surface or deep. Monitoring student progress throughout the learning journey on the learning intentions becomes one of the key functions of the I-PLC as teachers evaluate the impact of their teaching based on positive and negative evidence of student learning.

Key considerations in developing learning intentions are keeping the numbers of building blocks manageable and keeping the scope or size to a balance so that it does not microscope the progression to a point that the focus is so detailed that it balloons the number of learning intentions that are created that lead to the curricular aim (Popham, 2008). Key steps in creating the learning intentions begin with teachers gaining intimate knowledge about what the expectations of the broader curricular aim require both declaratively and procedurally. That is, what do students need to know and be able to do to reach mastery on the academic content standard or broader curricular aim. Next, teachers need to use backward planning to move from the broad aim to determine just exactly what important building blocks of subskills and enabling knowledge a student needs to learn to reach mastery of the broader curricular aim. These mapping sessions are more effectively carried out in the company of colleagues that teach parallel content. This is the power generated when the I-PLC process is embedded throughout TFM.

Next, teachers return to the measurability filter and apply it to all the building block learning intentions they identified. It makes little difference to identify a learning intention that is a diamond, only to have it turn into a piece of coal when we determine that there is no way to measure a student's status with that learning intention. It is important that this step is accomplished prior to moving to the last step when teachers actually sequence the building blocks in the order that they believe makes the most sense; that way, students actually move through the intentions on their way to the broader academic content standard (see figure 3.1).

Figure 3.1   Example Learning Intention

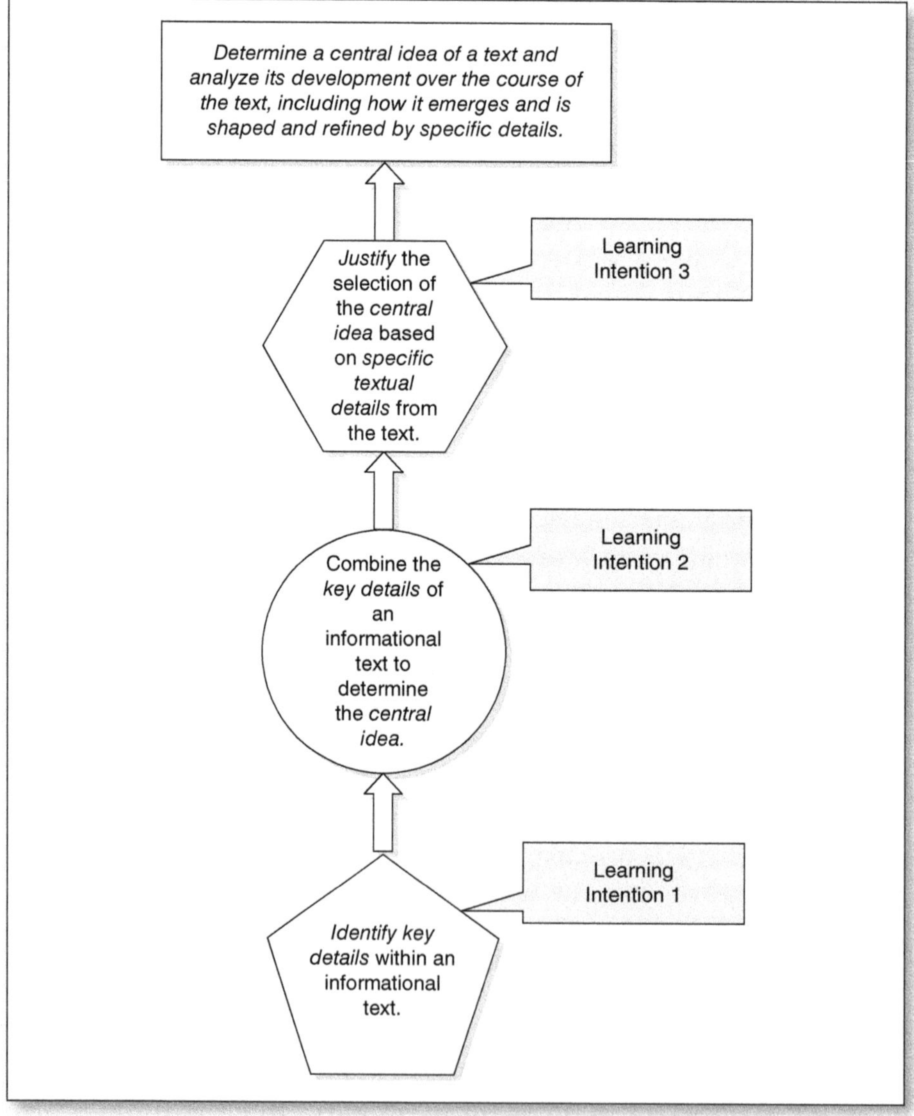

Source: CCSS, ELA.RI.6.2, 2010.

Another example is found in the Reading Standards for Informational Text 2 for the third grade:

Determine the main idea of a text; recount the key details and explain how they support the main idea. (CCSS, ELA, RI.3.2, p. 14)

Looking at this standard, the realization sets in that at the end of third grade, students are expected to know and be able to do several things. But there are also enabling skills and knowledge that students need in order to master these end of grade expectations. This enabling knowledge and skill set is what is referred to as a learning progression. In TFM, learning progressions house multiple learning intentions. In addition, these knowledge and skill requirements come in two flavors, or levels, those that require surface-level thinking, and those that require deep-level thinking. The following graphic organizer (see Table 3.2) easily captures how an I-PLCs works through the process of developing these learning intentions within the foundational steps of TFM.

In the example in Table 3.2, the surface knowledge represents the enabling knowledge (or learning intentions) that students need to achieve mastery as identified by a group of Grade 3 teachers working within the auspices of an I-PLC. A critical step for this group of educators is identifying just what it is that students are expected to know and be able to do in regard to learning outcomes. This is a critical first step of TFM's process.

Table 3.3 is an example of learning intentions for a math curricular aim, specifically found within the Common Core standards for math.

Table 3.2   Levels of Learning Intentions

Target Curricular Aim: *Determine the main idea of a text; recount the key details and explain how they support the main idea.*		
	Declarative	*Procedural*
Surface Level	Define the term: key detail. Define the term: main idea.	Using a piece of informational text, identify the key details.
Deep Level	Recount the key details of an informational text. Explain how key details are connected to the main idea.	Using a piece of informational text, synthesize the key details into the main idea.

Table 3.3   Learning Intentions Specific to a Math Curricular Aim

<table>
<tr><td colspan="3">Target Curricular Aim: Solve real-world and mathematical problems involving area, volume, and surface area of two- and three-dimensional objects composed of triangles, quadrilaterals, polygons, cubes, and right prisms.</td></tr>
<tr><td></td><td>Declarative</td><td>Procedural</td></tr>
<tr><td>Surface Level</td><td>Define the formula for the area of triangles, polygons, and cubes.

Define the formula for the volume of triangles, polygons, and cubes.</td><td>Use the formula for area to find the area of triangles, polygons, and cubes.

Use the formula for volume to find the area of triangles, polygons, and cubes.</td></tr>
<tr><td>Deep Level</td><td>Define the formula for area to find the area of quadrilaterals and right prisms.

Define the formula for volume to find the area of quadrilaterals and right prisms.</td><td>Use the formula for area of triangles, polygons, and cubes to solve real-world and mathematical problems.

Use the formula for volume of triangles, polygons, and cubes to solve real-world and mathematical problems.

Use the formula for area to find the area of quadrilaterals and right prisms and solve real-world and mathematical problems.

Use the formula for volume to find the area of quadrilaterals and right prisms and solve real-world and mathematical problems.</td></tr>
</table>

Source: CCSS, Math.7.G.6, 2010.

Making Curriculum Maps

Many teachers find it useful to chart this process for all the academic content standards that are the focus of a curricular unit. For some, this chart may cover a period lasting two to four weeks, a quarter's worth of instructional content, a semester, or even involve a diagram of learning intentions mapped to the curricular aims to cover for the year. To add some further organization to this map, I-PLCs may elect to include extra information for a learning intention, such as prelimi-nary decisions about how many class periods to devote to each learn-ing intention and what level of proficiency teachers need to see before adding or decreasing instructional time (Popham, 2008). This level of planning helps teachers develop a clearer picture of needed points for formative assessment, and anticipate any possible instructional decision changes that might occur as this real-time evidence is gathered on the students' status on the learning intentions. Ideally, the learning intentions in the curriculum map mark the key points in the instructional cycle when teachers want to formatively assess the status of students in regard to the learning targets. We discuss more about formative assessment in Chapter 5.

Making the Process Teacher-Driven

The true power of this process comes through the collaborative dialogue of professional educators intentionally selecting learning intentions for the focus of teaching and assessment. If possible, all teachers should play a role in these selections. In larger districts, representative groups of grade levels and content areas can make the initial selections of the learning intentions embedded in the broader curricular aims (academic content standards), but these drafts should go back to the other sites for feedback opportunities from colleagues. The representative groups use this feedback to finalize selections of the learning intentions which now characterize the significant curricular aims for that grade or course. Communication to everyone who provides input is vitally important to the rationale for the development of the learning intentions. Invaluable in the learning intention development process, is the teachers' subject area knowledge and understanding of the inherent learning progressions that occur across grades in the reaching of the broader curricular aims. What results is more clarity—clarity about how students advance from surface to deep learning within the journey of instruction and also more clarity based on student performance on pre-assessment when the students are entering the learning. Last, the identification of surface and deep learning intentions also provides the teachers clues as to the level of feedback necessary for students to be more effective learners. John Hattie (2012) found that teachers are able to give more effective feedback when the teacher knows a student's level of processing within the learning progression. Providing deep-level feedback to a student who is currently at the surface level of thinking can cause confusion and blank stares, while conversely, giving surface-level feedback to a student at a deeper level of knowing can produce boredom and can stifle the student's desire to move beyond his or her current level of understanding. Last, teachers must not forsake the importance of surface-level learning intentions for the deeper level. Both are important, and surface-level learning is critical for students to be able to relate and extend ideas beyond the surface level.

Monitoring the Effectiveness of Learning Intentions

Monitoring the effectiveness of learning intentions is an ongoing process. By making certain that a narrowed set of teaching and assessment goals are clearly articulated, educators are increasing the likelihood for success for all students in mastering these intentions. One of the largest effect sizes found in John Hattie's (2009) landmark research which is chronicled in the book *Visible Learning* pertain to this concept of "Teacher Clarity." Hattie found that the clarity of the teacher had an effect size of $d = 0.75$ on student achievement. Of the 138 influences studied by Hattie in his research, consider that this effect is nearly twice the mean effect size ($d = 0.40$). Accordingly, it becomes clear that the impact of clarity of learning intentions, and the success criteria (see Chapter 4) related to those priority curricular aims are well worth our attention as we seek to improve the achievement of students. Success of the learning intention development process should be measured in terms of student results. The monitoring of this process is deeply embedded in the actions of the I-PLC.

As they work through the formative assessment process, educators are constantly seeking evidence, both positive and negative, from students of their abilities in relation to the identified learning intentions. This formative assessment and, in turn, deep analysis of student strengths and weaknesses that may present obstacles to learning provides the information that teachers need to make real-time adjustments to strategies and also validate the inferences of student progress. Monitoring is a function of being able to infer the relative success, or lack thereof, of the strategies employed to teach the learning intentions. Since the focus of the formative analysis process and the I-PLC process is relative to student success on the learning intentions, monitoring is embedded at all levels of TFM.

The Efficacy of Learning Intentions

According to Doug Reeves (2011), the greatest gift that a school leader can give to the students and staff of a school is "focus." The development of clear learning intentions makes this focus come alive as educators work to make clear the success criteria for students. By unmistakably articulating the critical knowledge, skills, and dispositions that students need to be successful, schools take the mystery out of learning. In addition, they help ensure that the curriculum is implemented and, more importantly, consistent from one class to another providing educational equity for all students.

John Hattie (2012) found that individual teachers produced the greatest variance within a school's impact on student learning. Marzano (2003), in a similar analysis, found that a "Guaranteed and Viable Curriculum" had the number one impact on student achievement at the school level. That is, for students to have an equitable opportunity to learn and master subject matter, the content must be structured in a way that all students are guaranteed effective interactions with the content. Students and teachers need ample time to practice and deepen understanding of the content so that the curriculum is realistic based on the amount of time available for instruction (Marzano, 2003).

When teachers in the structured collaborative I-PLCs have ample time to teach, assess, evaluate, and reevaluate content as needed so that students have multiple opportunities for success, learning becomes the constant, and time is the variable that can be adjusted to meet students' most urgent needs. This is at the center of what TFM is all about: learning. Ideally this learning is ongoing for both students and adults.

Collaboration Is the Key

In the book *The Wisdom of Crowds,* James Surowiecki (2005) spoke to the great power leveraged by groups to solve complex problems. Surowiecki asserted that under the right conditions, groups make better decisions than singular individuals. A structured process for collaboration allows groups to consider multiple solutions, see different sides of situations with more clarity, and thus more deeply examine the critical "ups and downs" of various choices. The major supposition purported by the book is that organizations are "better off entrusting structured collaborative groups with major decisions rather than leaving them in the hands of one or two people, no matter how smart those people are" (Surowiecki, 2005, p. 31).

Others touting the importance of using effective collaboration include Richard DuFour, Rebecca DuFour, and Robert Eaker. In summarizing the research on the importance of using structured collaboration in schools in the book *Revisiting Professional Learning Communities at Work: New Insights for Improving Schools,* the DuFours and Eaker (2008) came to the conclusion that "isolation is the enemy of school improvement" (p. 177). Roland Barth (2006), Phillip Schlechty (2005), and Richard Elmore (2006) all support the need for effective structured collaborative processes in schools for the schools to reach their true potential.

All the processes included within TFM are founded on the premise that true school improvement must be teacher-driven. With extensive on-site coaching and development, using the collaborative decision-making structure of the I-PLC process, teachers, school leaders, and support staff are taught how to apply structured collaborative protocols to develop learning intentions, create success criteria, and complete a formative analysis of students ongoing learning. True structured collaboration is the vehicle that drives the model to reach and sustain success.

Communicating Learning Intentions

One of the most critical attributes of learning intentions is that they have to be communicated to and internalized by students. One of the critical steps in engaging students in learning is ensuring that students are well aware of the intended learning outcomes of the activities that they are engaged in during the course of classroom interaction. Overexuberant superfluous activity in a classroom means very little if students do not understand what they are learning. One valuable way that teachers can communicate the all-important outcomes of learning is by using the WALT (see Figure 3.3) acronym to cue students into what they are learning. WALT stands for "We Are Learning To . . ."

Here is another example of the WALT acronym posted on a board in the classroom:

We Are Learning To . . .

- Determine the main idea of text.
- Use math to solve real-world problems.
- Write persuasively.
- Use a topographical map.
- Develop an effective speech.
- Perform a back summersault.
- Differentiate between the various forms of government.

Figure 3.4   WALT's

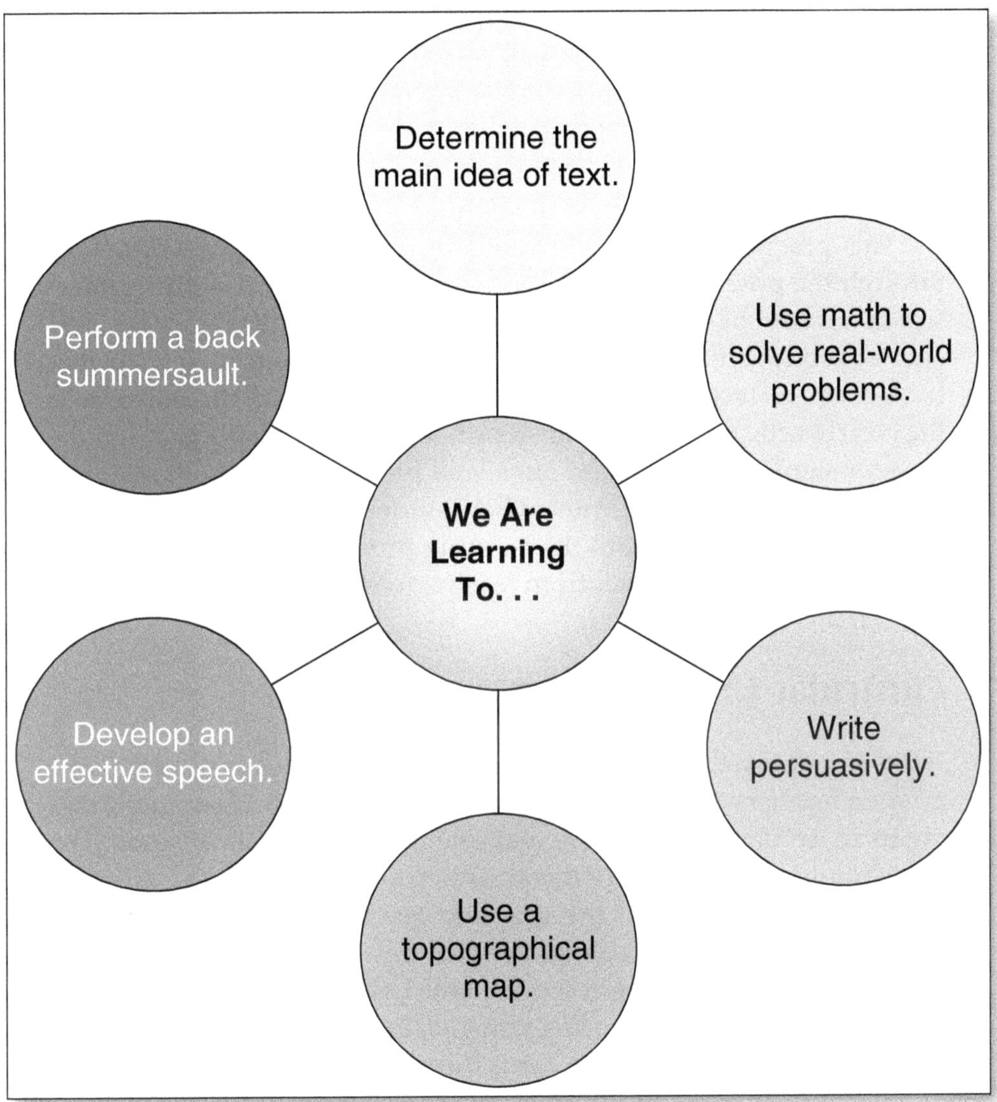

All of the examples are the worthwhile learning intentions that teachers create to support the development of the needed knowledge and skills that students require for success in school. It is very important that students know what it is that they are learning, and in addition, know what it means to master that intention. The success criteria defines what it is students need to know and be able to do in order to be considered proficient on the learning intentions. The learning intentions and success criteria work together like *hand and glove* to help students and teachers create clarity around what is to be learned and, even more important, what students should be knowing, doing, and saying as they work through the learning journey to reach proficiency. In Chapter 4, we discuss the development of success criteria and delve deeper into their relationship to learning intentions. For now, the goal is to recognize the essential first step of TFM I-PLC is to clearly derive, from the academic content standards, the critical learning intentions that students need for success in learning.

This practice may seem arduous in the beginning; nevertheless, through the power of collaboration drawing on the collective professional wisdom of colleagues, teachers can achieve this necessary first step to produce this all important learning intention road map that leads from surface- to deep-level learning. In the end, the outcome is the clearly articulated learning steps needed for students to reach the broader significant curricular aims, and the clarity that both students and teachers need to determine where students are entering the learning. This information about the learning process allows for the application of effective feedback from teacher to student, and vice versa.

Curricular Units of Study

A last key step in the process of the identification of learning intentions is when teachers then group these intentions to curriculum maps that organize similar or cross curricular intentions into units of study. The curriculum unit is a common convention of grouping like curricular outcomes (in this case at the granular level of learning intentions), into manageable organized instructional time frames normally lasting anywhere from two to eight weeks. This helps frame intended learning for planning formative assessments, instruction, and summative assessment. It can also help to focus the work of the I-PLC for the sake of root cause analysis and the ongoing search for the impact of educators' innovations aimed at learning.

KEY CONSIDERATIONS

It is only when we collaboratively narrow the scope of the curricular aims and we deeply commit to teaching and assessing, that we can make the job of ensuring success for all students a reality. Developing explicit learning intentions is a key step in creating clarity around the knowledge that all kids need to know and the skill set required to accomplish the tasks. This means that we are making a commitment to ensure that we intentionally design the curriculum so that students have sufficient time to be introduced properly to new content, engage in deliberate practice with this content, and then generate and test their understandings of the critical content so that they can be successful in college and careers.

Guiding Questions

1. Were teachers in every class clear about what they were teaching this past year in your school/district? Were the students clear on what was taught?

2. How did teachers decide what was taught and what was not?

3. Have teachers within your school/district made determinations about what content is most critical for student success?

4. How does the idea of creating clarity for teachers and students about what is being taught make sense?

5. How could teachers benefit from working with colleagues to make determinations about what is most important and about what enabling knowledge and skills students need to master to be successful?

4

Criteria for Success

Setting a goal is not the main thing. It is deciding how you will go about achieving it and staying with that plan.

Tom Landry

Why Success Criteria?

According to *Merriam-Webster's Online Dictionary*, success is "the correct or desired result of an attempt." Criterion (criteria in the singular) is defined as "something that is used as a reason for making a judgment or decision" (Merriam-Webster, 2014b). In the context of learning, when we put the two words together to form a success criteria, we establish a marker or foundation to judge whether the desired learning intention is achieved to the level of quality sufficient to meet the goal. Learning intentions and success criteria work in concert so that teachers and students reach clarity about three things: what needs to be learned, how the learning is progressing, and once learning is measured, what are the next steps for both teachers and students in the learning process (see Figure 4.1).

Support for Success Criteria

Though we are discussing success criteria as it relates to the attainment of desired learning outcomes in education, success criteria are appreciated in many other disciplines as well. The following is Microsoft's

Figure 4.1   Learning Intentions, Success Criteria, and Clarity

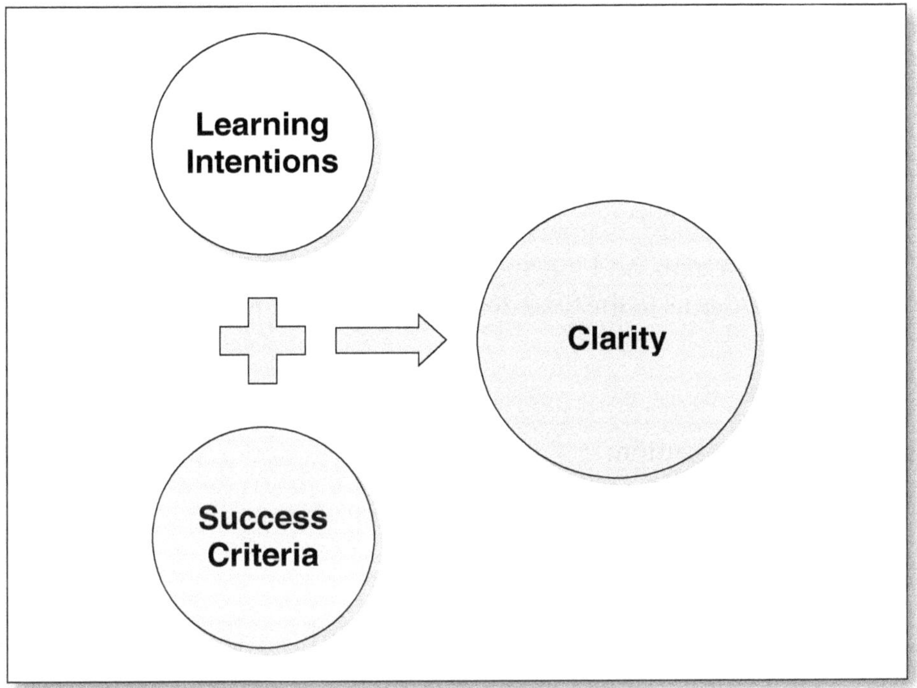

take on the importance of clear success criteria: "The project success criteria can then be derived by answering the question, 'How do I know I've done a great job?' Just checking off tasks on the project schedule isn't enough. The success criteria speaks to the quality of the completed job and specifics about how the goals are met" (Suchan, 2014). Correspondingly, Wiegers (2002) also speaks to the importance of success criteria by stating, "Defining explicit success criteria during the project's inception phase keeps stakeholders focused on shared objectives and establishes targets for evaluating progress . . . Well-written success criteria are feasible, quantified, and verifiable." Both of these business giants recognize the importance of having a clear comprehension of progress. Hattie (2012) stated that one of the greatest hindrances to learning can be an inadequate definition of what progress looks like in regard to learning. Clarity in defining this key concept opens up the likelihood of more informed instructional decisions and more powerfully effective feedback. Importantly, teachers should not be the only ones to hold the common concept of progress. The ideal goal is the formulation of learning intentions and success criteria achieved in such a manner that the students also internalize these clarifiers of learning. The ultimate goal of this exercise is that as students gain mastery of the surface-level aspects and develop deeper conceptual understandings of the content under study, the students also develop the ability to utilize clarity of the success criteria to develop self-regulation in learning and self-feedback.

Hand and Glove

The relationship between learning intentions and success criteria is very straightforward. Namely, the learning intention sets the target like a location on a map, and the success criteria is an effective set of directions that guides us to the final destination. Let's look at some examples:

Example 1

Learning Intention:

- Identify key details in an informational text.

Success Criterion:

- Using a highlighter or other identification tactic, the student can identify the key details within an informational text.

Example 2

Learning Intention:

- Determine the central idea of an informational text.

Success Criteria:

- After reading an informational text, the student can successfully identify the key details using a highlighter or other identification tactic.
- After analyzing an informational text, the student is able to synthesize the key details of an informational text into a central idea.
- The student is able to justify his or her choice of central idea with specific textual evidence.

Example 3

Learning Intention:

- Use textual evidence to support how the central idea develops within a text.

Success Criterion:

- After reading an informational text, the student determines the central idea and then, in addition, justifies that selection with textual evidence, either orally or in writing.

As you can see from the preceding examples, defined success criteria provide both the teacher and student a guide for what a student needs to know or be able to do if the student attains the learning intention. In addition, the level of response expected in the learning intention should match the same level of cognitive processing in the success criteria. If the student's response fails to match the level of thinking articulated in the learning intention as defined by the success criteria, then students and teachers are provided essential information that can have implications for instruction, metacognition, and feedback. Also, the level of student response in relationship to the success criteria also informs teachers and students of where the student is entering the learning apropos of the knowledge or skill to master, or in relation to the enabling knowledge and skill needed for proficiency. Notice that instead of a single success criterion for the second example of a learning intention, there is a progression of the success criteria toward the realization of the learning intention. As shown in Example 2, teachers can use the success criteria to differentiate student attainment of the learning intention by keeping the learning intention constant for all students, but scaffolding the success criteria. Finally, success criteria can also be used to measure progress against a learning intention. Figure 4.2 illustrates that if the following learning intention was defined by all three of the success criteria in a progression (as identified by the I-PLC), teachers can see if students are at the surface level of thinking with this learning intention, or at the deeper levels of goal, and beyond.

This example shows how teachers can differentiate success criteria for measurement purposes to help determine where students enter the learning progression regarding this particular learning intention. In addition, as stated earlier, ascertaining where students are in their thinking is also critical for planning first and next steps in instruction, both for teachers and for students.

What Is the Level of Thinking?

To make certain that the identified knowledge and skills are being taught at the appropriate levels of cognitive load and rigor, it is important that educators take the time to consider what the action

Figure 4.2 Learning Intentions and Success Criteria

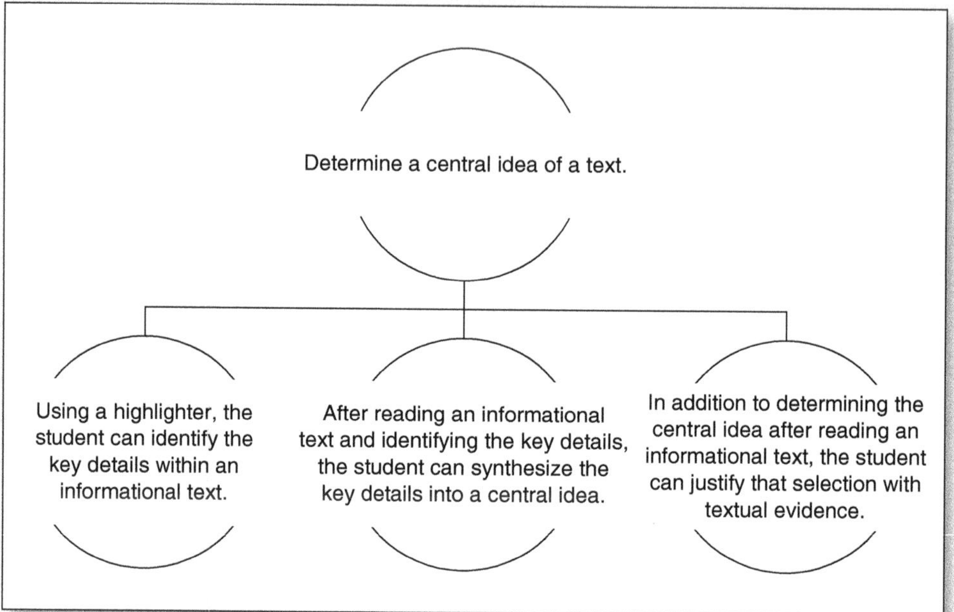

verb (the skill) is directing toward the noun or noun phrase (the conceptual or declarative knowledge) within the learning intention derived from the academic content standard. One of the common ways that educators can do this is by referring to Webb's Depth of Knowledge, or DOK, the process and criteria developed by Dr. Norman Webb (1997) for examining alignment of academic content standards and standardized assessments. Originally designed to determine if a standardized test and an academic content standard require the same levels of thinking or rigor (depth of knowledge), these criteria can also be useful for designing classroom tasks and assessments that ensure appropriate alignment to the expectations of the academic content standards (Webb, 1997). In essence, the DOK level describes the kind of thinking required of the student when engaged in the task:

- Does the task require surface-level thinking, normally associated with a DOK 1; or
- Does the required level extend the surface-level understanding to include more of the application level, DOK 2; or
- Is the task at the level of synthesis and meta-cognition, at DOK Level 3 or 4?

Many times we can assess these levels of understanding and thinking with students by asking three simple questions:

1. What do you know? (Recall and Reproduction)

2. What can you do with it? (Skills, Concepts, and Application)

3. What can you teach others? (Extended thinking and Metacognition)

The reason that this process is so important is that now teachers can use this coding as a guide to construct engaging tasks and assessment items with the confidence that they will be aligned to the spirit and the rigor intended within the learning intentions derived from the standards. This process is more readily done through collaboration, because a consensus approach should be used to determine the levels of thinking of the tasks and curricular aims (in the same manner as academic content standard). For example, in the case of this language arts learning intention in Figure 4.2, some teachers may believe that the thinking required for students to complete the identified task (determining the central idea of an informational text) is based on the second success criteria at a level of 2 on Webb's DOK. Others might argue that since the student is determining the central idea, and in the case of the final learning intention, justifying the selection with textual evidence, such a response is equivalent to a DOK level of 3, which requires more extended thinking and synthesis. In this case, what we have just done is not only apply the level of DOK to the task, but also to the response. This concept is foreign to many familiar with Bloom's taxonomy and Webb's DOK levels because Bloom's, and for the most part Webb's DOK, have always presupposed that the verb selected for the task elicits a response of students at the level prescribed by the verb. Hattie and Purdie (1998) make this case in their support for the SOLO taxonomy developed by Biggs and Collis (1982).

SOLO Taxonomy, derived from the **S**tructure of the **O**bserved **L**earning **O**utcomes, provides "a means of classifying learning outcomes in terms of their complexity, enabling us to assess students' work in terms of its *quality* not of how many bits of this and of that they got right" (Biggs, n.d.).

There are five levels related to the taxonomy. The first level is the *prestructural level,* which relates to the belief that students do not have any grasp of the ideas related to the targeted curricular aims; thus, the term *prestructural* signifies that students presently have no structure on which to build higher levels of complexity of thinking. The second level in the taxonomy is called the *unistructural level* because in this level the student has the complexity of understanding of a solitary idea in relation to the larger curricular aim or construct. Verbs and phrases associated with this level are the following: *identify, name, and follow a simple procedure.* As one can see, there is some relation to Bloom's (2001) lower levels and even Webb's (1997) DOK chart when looking at the level of processing with these verbs. The biggest difference is that both Bloom's levels and Webb's DOK place much more focus on the complexity of the task and the alignment of the task to the curricular aim or academic content standard whereas the SOLO taxonomy is also concerned with the complexity of the student response. If we ask a student to determine the central idea of a text, and if that student gives us a response at the unistructural level, the student might be able to give us a key detail of the text, but not much more. The third level in the SOLO taxonomy is the *multistructural level.* This moves the complexity from a single idea to a grasp of multiple ideas in relation to the curricular aim. Some verbs and phrases associated with this level are *combine, describe, enumerate,* and *perform serial skills.* Again note the similarities and differences in the verbs long associated with Bloom's, specifically that the SOLO taxonomy does not presuppose that just because the task has the verb present that it elicits a response on par with that expectation. SOLO recognizes that students' responses can vary across a broad continuum of the five levels represented in the SOLO taxonomy. An example at the multistructural level of complexity in thinking is when a student moves from being able to understand the concept of a single key detail in a text, to the understanding that many key details in the text can be coalesced into a central idea. Moving higher still in the SOLO taxonomy, we move to the *relational level.* This is when students now are able to relate the ideas to other ideas. Verbs and phrases associated with this level are *analyze, apply, argue, compare/contrast, criticize, explain causes (cause and effect), relate,* and *justify.* Observe that this level of student response relates to the higher levels of the works of both Bloom and Webb. For example, a student at this level is not only able to coalesce the key details of a text into the central idea; the student can also justify his or her selection with textual evidence from the text in question or even other texts he or she has read. This certainly ups the ante in the response that the student is able to provide. This goes beyond simply being able to determine the central idea exemplified in the multistructural level. Finally, at the highest level of the SOLO taxonomy we find the *extended abstract level.* The following verbs are associated with this level: *create, formulate, generate, hypothesize, reflect,* and *theorize.* Continuing with the example of determining the central idea of a text, if a student is able to theorize how the central idea might change based on the addition or the deletion of certain key details, this requires students to think beyond the information that is provided. According to the SOLO taxonomy, this is the highest level of cognitive processing we can expect from a student. Figure 4.3 is a summary of the five levels of the SOLO taxonomy.

As you look at the figure, note how these statements also differentiate the common task of determining the central idea, a common expectation in the Common Core Standards (2010). This provides teachers a way to use a common learning intention discussed in Chapter 3, while at the same time applying differentiated success criteria to gauge where students are in the learning. This is a concrete way that teachers can plan differentiation within the same classroom for students on the same learning intention by crafting learning intentions and success criteria in this manner. Once teachers determine where students are on the continuum of the learning

Figure 4.3   Examples of SOLO Taxonomy and Determining Central Idea Learning Outcome

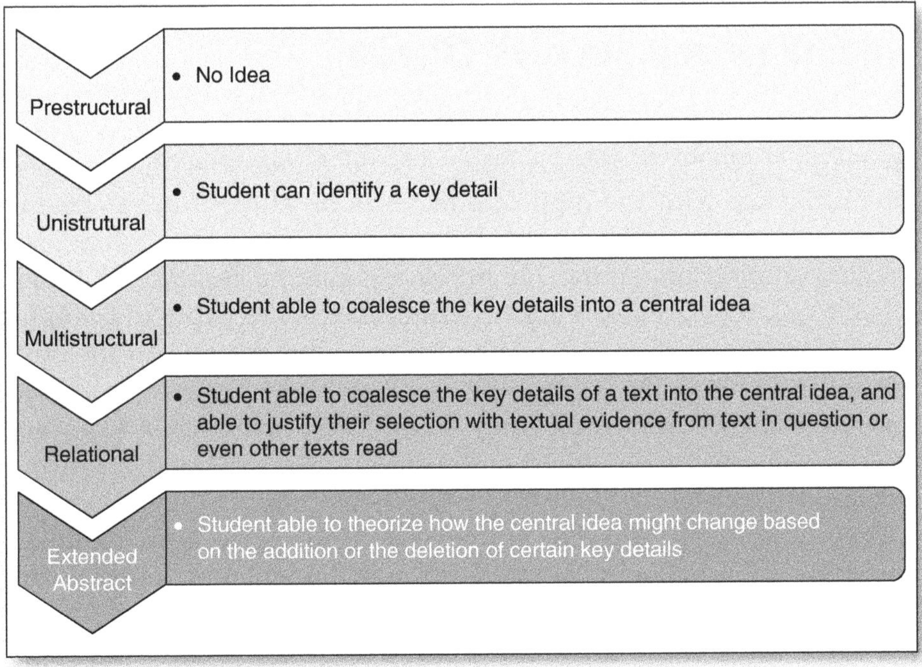

taxonomy, the recommendation is that they provide instruction and formative feedback at the level needed to challenge students to progress to the level of their thinking. Hattie (2012) states that "the key is to provide instruction sufficiently above the current student level and aiming to move the student '+1' in their learning progression" (p. 111). Providing instruction and feedback on a lower level can stifle students' progress, whereas providing instruction and feedback two or three levels above can go right over their heads.

Learning intentions and success criteria are as important for teachers as they are for students. They help both students and teachers understand what they are learning and their current level of cognitive processing within the learning. This knowledge also provides valuable information for both teachers and students for the next steps. Formative assessment (see Chapter 5) is a critical component of this process as well. Finally, the power of collaboration in the form of professional learning communities concerned with determining impact, such as the I-PLCs, is another critical part of the effective use of the learning intentions, success criteria, and formative assessment. The inclusion of these four powerful foundational practices in TFM support the efficacy of the model as a powerful tool for driving continuous improvement cycles for all schools.

Efficacy of Using Learning Intentions and Success Criteria

In the largest educational research study to date that is recorded in Hattie's (2009) *Visible Learning,* Hattie found that the number one influence with the highest effect size on student achievement is what he termed *Self-Reported Grades* ($d = 1.44$). This effect size ranked number one of the 138 influences that he studied. The idea of self-reported grades is that when students are explicitly taught metacognitive strategies of self-assessment and designs for the next steps for learning, the impact is equivalent to 3.6 years of academic growth! Teacher communication of learning intentions and success criteria are critical for students developing the skill of assessment capability. (Hattie, 2009, 2012) Only when students internalize the targets of learning, and the common definition of progress on those targets, which is communicated through the success criteria, can students hope to reach the level of metacognition that Hattie defines as assessment capability. Hattie (2012, p. 141) identifies these students as *Assessment Capable Learners*.

Communicating Success Criteria

Essential to students gaining the knowledge and skill they need to become assessment capable is the effective communication of the learning intentions and success criteria by teachers. This goes far beyond the simple posting of the learning intentions and success criteria on a board in the classroom. This process of communication should include direct instruction and periodic monitoring with students to determine the students' understanding of the intentions and success criteria for the intended learning. In addition, Shirley Clarke (2005) and others advocate for direct student involvement in the development and definition of the success criteria from the outset. Certainly teachers should ensure that the learning intentions and success criteria are communicated in language assessable to all students. This includes considerations for students with disabilities and English Language Learners (ELLs).

Using exemplars of student work also helps students internalize the success criteria. This can be done by teachers to help students better define and operationalize what is meant by the learning intention. Having this work posted in a rubric format that illustrates student thinking from prestructural level through to the extended abstract level can help students visualize the linguistic success criteria. In addition, this display also helps prompt students to the level of thinking that is required to go above their current level of understanding. This goes back to the "plus 1" principle discussed earlier. In other words, we want to apply positive pressure on the current status level of a student to promote and encourage a trajectory of progress to higher levels of thinking. This requires knowing at what level students are presently thinking and having a clear concept of levels of understanding beyond a student's current status. This clarity is achieved first with the teacher or teachers across the course or grade level, and then this model can be shared as a part of instruction with the ultimate goal that students can internalize and become self-directed in their learning. As Hattie (2012) concluded, this does not happen with the "guide on the side" type of teaching (p. 19). It takes direct and engaged instruction provided on behalf of teachers for students to reach this level of function. Thus, clear learning intentions are doubly important, for teachers first and then for students.

KEY CONSIDERATIONS

The first step in clarifying learning intentions is developing success criteria that define the essential knowledge, skills, and dispositions that students need to learn to successfully show mastery on those learning intentions. In so doing, educators can identify the success criteria that make up the knowledge, skills, and dispositions that we hope endure for students long after instruction. Success criteria answer the question, "What does success look like on this learning intention?" The sharing and communication of these intentions with students should be an intentional part of the instructional process. As students are better able to internalize the learning intentions and success criteria, the stage is set for the ability of students to self- and peer-assess. All these processes are foundational elements to TFM that at its core is about improving teaching and learning.

Guiding Questions

1. How have teachers in your school or district identified specifically what students need to know and be able to do to achieve success within the standards, learning progressions, or learning intentions?

2. How are teachers currently ensuring that students learn the deeper concepts implicit within the standards?

3. Do teachers align instruction, assessment, and classroom tasks to the standards? How do we know there is alignment? How do we interpret student responses to tasks to determine the level of thinking students are exhibiting?

4. How are learning and intentions related?

5. Who should use learning intentions and success criteria throughout the course of learning?

5

Formative Analysis

Formative assessment exists for exactly one reason: To enhance students' learning.

W. James Popham

Key Questions for Professional Learning Communities

Leading up to this chapter, we answered only one of the four important guiding questions that should direct the work of any effective professional learning community, specifically, "What is it that we want all of our students to know and be able to do?" We began answering this question in Chapter 3 when we discussed learning intentions, which represent the enabling knowledge and skill required with a learning progression that is developed directly from the broader expectations commonly referred to in the United States as academic content standards. In Chapter 4, we further clarified and operationalized the learning intentions by providing clear success criteria that defines specifically what these intended learning outcomes are by describing the markers of success that point to actionable behaviors that students exhibit when they reach the learning intentions. The second critical question that professional learning communities seek to answer is, "How do we know if our students have achieved the intended learning outcomes?" The answer to this question actually began with the development of clear success criteria in Chapter 4, but we elaborate on our answer to this question in this chapter as we discuss the third foundational practice in TFM—formative assessment or formative analysis.

What Is Formative Assessment?

As educators continue to engage in learning the intricacies of assessment, they have only scratched the surface of the capabilities of the effective use of assessment-elicited evidence. Although strides have been made, unfortunately we still live in an age when assessments are primarily used for the practice of "naming, shaming, and blaming." This reality prompts a fair question: Are we truly using assessments to the fullest potential in our endeavors to improve student achievement? In many cases, the answer is no we are not. Currently, if you polled the majority of your colleagues in your school or district as to why they use assessments, you will undoubtedly find that a majority of those well-meaning colleagues answer, "to assign student grades." That is, in the recent past, educators relied primarily on summative assessment.

Summative assessment is assessment that serves to measure where a student is on the learning journey at any point in time. Results from this type of assessment are used for many worthwhile reasons, such as assigning student grades, meeting No Child Left Behind (NCLB; 2002) requirements, and even determining graduation status in some states (U.S. Department of Education, 2002). Even though summative assessment has merit, it is not the type of assessment that has shown the most promise in fostering improvements in student achievement; that distinction goes to summative assessment's formative brethren.

According to assessment expert W. J. Popham (2014), multiple research studies indicate that the type of assessment with the distinction of being an instructionally embedded technique with the power to improve student achievement is formative assessment. Popham goes on to define formative assessment as follows:

> Formative assessment is a planned process in which assessment-elicited evidence of students' status is used by teachers to adjust their ongoing instructional procedures or by students to adjust their current learning tactics. (2014, p. 290)

In looking at Popham's definition, many important nuances are apparent. One key point that leads to quite a bit of confusion is the fact that formative assessment does not refer to any particular instrument, it is much more about the process of how we go about using the assessment-elicited evidence that we gather. Many wrongheaded colleagues might be overheard defining this or that test as a formative assessment. Please do not succumb to such sloppy labeling. Because the term formative assessment was applied so loosely, many prominent researchers stopped using the term altogether. In an effort to emphasize more completely what is done with the evidence from any particular evidence gathering enterprise, TFM refers to the concept of formative assessment as *formative analysis*. The hope is that this term prompts practitioners to remember that formative assessment is not about any instrument, but it is much more about the interpretations that teachers and students make with the results of assessment.

Looking back to the definition of formative assessment, there are two persons who can take action regarding the evidence generated in the formative analysis process. Teachers can certainly make instructional adjustments in response to formative evidence, and ideally they do. However, as discussed earlier in reference to John Hattie's (2009, 2012) work, the most powerful use of formative evidence results when students use this information to make adjustment in the strategies they are employing to learn. In addition to knowing the learning intentions, and where the student's present performance is in relation to these learning intentions and success criteria, the gold standard is a student who uses this information to become self-directed in formulating next steps for learning.

Since the work of Black and Wiliam in 1998, we have known for some time the power that the strategy of formative assessment can have in the classroom. Black and Wiliam found that when used effectively, the strategy of formative assessment can have a significant effect size (effect size $d = .40–.70$). An effect size is a metric used by statisticians to compare the effects in different studies for more ease of comparison. John Hattie (2009) found that the average effect size of the 138 influences that he studied in his work chronicled in the book *Visible Learning* was an effect size of $d = .40$. Robert Coe (2002) stated that "effect size is a simple way of quantifying the difference between two groups . . ." Through extensive research, Hattie was able to relate the effect size of $d = .40$ to 1 year's worth of academic growth. Thus, Black and Wiliam found that formative assessment, when the strategy is used with fidelity, has the potential for promoting nearly 2 years' worth of academic growth in students. The critical point here is that formative assessment is a *means* to an *end*: to formatively analyze evidence, to make more valid inferences, to provide much needed information to make better informed, real-time instructional decisions. Again, ideally both teachers and students are using this evidence to consider next steps for teaching and learning.

Hattie (2012) found that *Providing Formative Evaluation,* with its effect size of $d = .90$, was tied for fourth in his list of 150 different influences. The fact that a great deal of research supports the position that what is effective for student learning is also effective in adult learning causes this author to reason that the reverse of that finding is also true. If providing formative evaluation to adults about their practice has a significant impact on achievement, can't we have more impact if we provide students rapid formative feedback about their learning process as well? In addition, Hattie reported the effect size for Response to Intervention as $d = 1.07$, and used this influence to frame all the protocols where "teachers are talking to teachers about teaching" (2012, p. 60). Herein lies the difference between simply giving a common formative assessment and using its results to make cursory teaching adjustments versus actually going further *and deeper by using formative analysis.*

The key in formative analysis is that educators are measuring the effectiveness of their strategies by the results evident in the pre-planned collections of student work and assessment tasks. According to Hattie (2012), "The teacher must know when learning is occurring or not . . ." (p. 17), and once this information is attained then determine what the most cogent next steps to promote growth are. Last, through structured educator collaboration, based on the results of formative pre- and post-assessments, real-time decisions are made to meet the needs of students combined with planned and periodic formative comprehension strategies. According to the research that supports their use, it is essential to this approach that formative assessment practices require fidelity so that these assessments, no matter how informal, must be planned. One of the areas of confusion with the formative assessment process is that many teachers espouse that they are already *doing* formative assessment as they use strategies to check student understanding when teaching. The problem with this assertion is that for any type of assessment to yield valid inferences about a subject variable, planning, a clarifying purpose, and the appropriate assessment task is required. All of these help yield the evidence needed to elicit the appropriate evidence necessary to reveal student status on the variable. Without proper planning and forethought before the process ever begins, these results are not possible (Popham, 2014).

The three main pillars supporting the foundation of formative analysis are purpose, evidence, and inference (see Figure 5.1). What do we want to know about student learning? What covert variable are we interested in learning more about by eliciting some evidence through a formative assessment? Evidence seeking is the true goal in the formative assessment process. In this formative analysis, we are in a continuous cycle of seeking evidence related to a student's status on some educational variable of interest and the impact of the adult strategies that we, as educators, employ in an effort to influence these variables. Last, the goal for educational assessment is to make valid inferences about student abilities. James Popham (2003) stated,

> Educational measurement is, at bottom, an *inference-making enterprise* in which we formally collect overt, test-based evidence from students to arrive at what we hope are accurate inferences about students' status with respect to covert, educationally important variables: reading ability, knowledge of history, etc. (p. 4)

Formative analysis at its core is about making valid inferences about student understanding or ability by looking at evidence of student performance. This is most effectively done through structured collaboration using the I-PLC process discussed in detail in Chapter 7. The initial step is to make certain that we are very clear

Figure 5.1   Three Keys to Formative Analysis

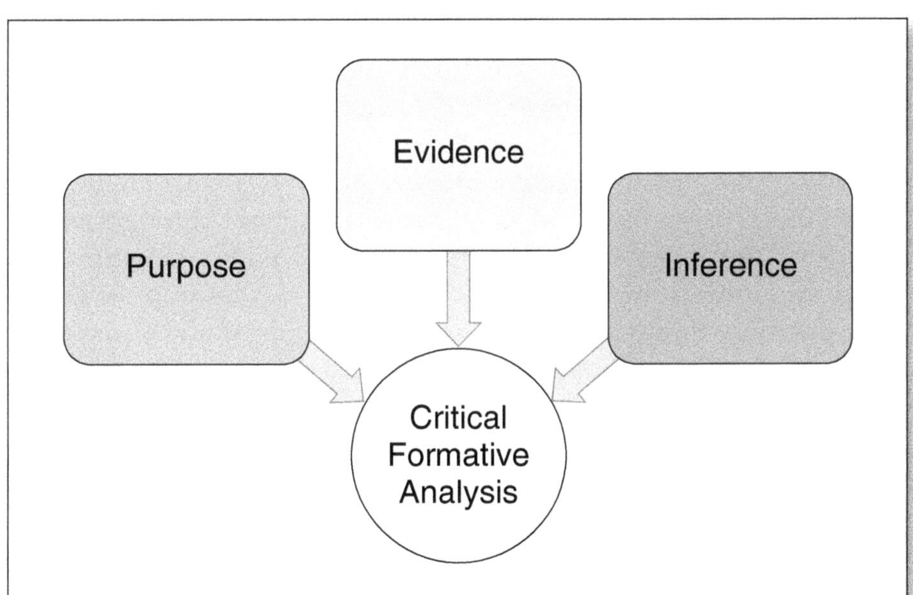

about the purpose of the assessment to ensure that we use the appropriate tools to collect evidence and make valid inferences. Popham (2003) stated, "The accuracy of these inferences is critical, because a teacher's understanding of students' knowledge, abilities, and attitudes should form the basis for the teacher's instructional decisions" (p. 5). In other words, invalid inferences can lead to less than stellar instructional decisions.

Hattie (2012) makes it very clear that when we use evidence to provide effective feedback (effect size $d = .75$), provide formative evaluation (effect size $d = .90$), and move students to the point where they become self-regulated learners (Hattie uses the term where they are achieving "self-reported grades/assessment capabilities" [effect size $d = 1.44$]), we have the potential for unprecedented improvements in student achievement and success. This evidence and the resulting inferences help teachers make decisions about the following:

1. The nature and purpose of curriculum.

2. The students' prior knowledge.

3. How long to teach something.

4. The effectiveness of instruction. (Popham, 2003, pp. 5–6)

All of these decisions are crucial for effective instruction and ensuring that students receive instruction targeted to meet their needs specific to where they are presently in the journey of learning. Hattie (2012) stated, "The excellent teacher must be diligent about what is working and what is not working in the classroom" (p. 17). Educators can use structured collaboration to ensure that this targeted instruction based on student strengths and obstacles is addressed across all classrooms, schools, and the entire system when they couple this effective formative analysis with the process of I-PLCs. The goal of TFM is to create alignment throughout the system on fewer priorities that are monitored with a common language and understanding. Consequently at the classroom level, the goals are more tightly aligned to learning intentions and success criteria; however, as we move to the school and system levels, there can be different types of goals and performance-based monitors, but the adaptability of the I-PLC process remains as a powerful method to conduct evidence-driven decision making at all levels. This process also helps to promote an aligned language of learning across the system.

When discussing alignment, Aryn Karpinski and Jerome D'Agostino (2013) report the following key elements for formative assessment in the book *The International Guide to Student Achievement:*

1. Identification of learning goals *(learning intentions)*, outcomes, and criteria for achievement *(success criteria).*

2. Communication between teachers and students about students' current knowledge status and future directions.

3. Active Involvement of students in their own learning.

4. Teachers responding to feedback by modifying teaching strategies. (p. 202)

The processes involved with both formative analysis and TFM address each one of these listed attributes thereby providing the level of impact possible through the harnessing of the true power of formative assessment as supported by the research.

A Little More on Assessment Lingo

According to Black and Wiliam (1998), the most common use of assessment in schools is the assigning of marks or grades. This, of course, is a worthwhile exercise and required in many cases, but as indicated by the work of Popham (2003, 2014), Black and Wiliam (1998, 2009) and Hattie (2012), this form of summative assessment is not the most powerful use of assessment when it comes to improving student achievement. Summative assessment is primarily employed to ascertain what students know or do not know at a designated point in time (Garrison & Ehringhaus, 2007). Examples include state exams, semester exams, and district benchmark tests. The explanation as to whether an assessment or test is summative or formative is derived from what educators or students do with the evidence and information received from analyzing the assessment. If we, as educators, do not use the information to impact what we do within the course of learning (whether as adults or students), the assessment is considered summative.

Formative assessment on the other hand, according to Garrison and Ehringhaus (2007), is part of the instructional process. Anytime a teacher gathers evidence from students to adjust and improve teaching and learning, that process is considered a formative assessment. James Popham (2003, 2014) strongly suggests that this evidence gathering should be planned in advance to make it more systematic and to ensure that we have a structured process to provide accountability. That is, it is not enough for us as educators to simply say, "Certainly I use evidence to guide my instruction." These formative assessments should be planned beforehand to ensure that we define the exact purpose of the assessment and are very clear about the specific evidence that we are seeking in relation to a specific variable, for example, reading comprehension, ability to draw inferences, ability to multiply two-digit numbers, and so on. This specificity is vital if we are to make valid inferences. The validity of our inferences is critical because in formative analysis, we use this information to identify student strengths and weaknesses in learning. Based on the identified levels of student processing, we then collaboratively select strategies directly related to addressing student needs (i.e., when intervention is called for and/or extending student learning when students demonstrate proficiency).

Both formative and summative assessments have a place in an effective assessment system, but the position of TFM is that to improve student achievement, formative assessment is where educators should consign their focus (see Figure 5.2). As we seek evidence and examples of what students know and can do, it is agreed that both summative assessment and formative assessment are important to developing the complete picture. But when it comes to improving

Figure 5.2   Unbalanced Assessment

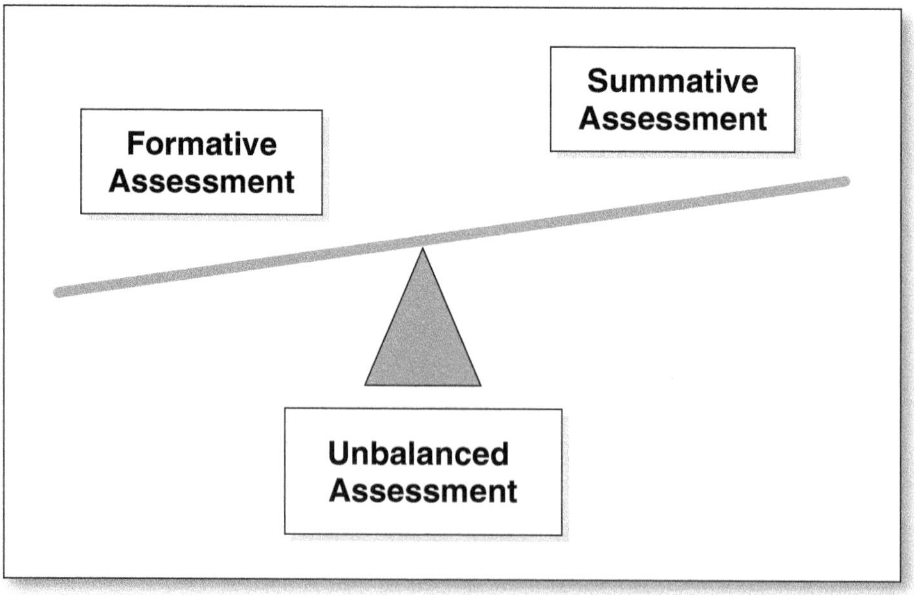

student achievement, formative assessment far outpaces summative assessment in this regard. It is for this reason that the author differs from others that might lobby for a balanced assessment system. For the benefit of learning, an unbalanced system in favor of formative assessment actually rules the day. As a matter of fact, Black and Wiliam (2009) recommend as many as two to five formative assessments per week to help teachers gather evidence of student learning and to inform instructional decision making. Ideally, students become actively engaged in the process to the point that they can clearly articulate the target for learning (the learning intention), where they are presently in relation to this learning target (status in relation to success criteria), and what next steps (adjustments in learning tactics) they might take to reach this target. Unbalanced assessment then is essential to assessment directed toward improving student and teacher learning—formative assessment should be occurring more often than summative assessment is.

Aligning Assessment Items to Learning Intentions and Success Criteria

The systematic nature of TFM takes us back to the learning intentions and success criteria in the development of aligned and effective formative assessments. For example, we use an example of a learning intention and the differentiated success criteria from in the previous chapter:

Learning Intention(s)

- Determine the central idea of an informational text.

Success Criteria

- After reading an informational text, the student identifies the key details.
- The student synthesizes the key details into a central idea.
- The student can justify the choice of the central idea selected with textual evidence.

Ideally the success criteria prompts the development of assessment items that are ideal for gauging student status regarding both the learning intentions and the success criteria.

In constructing such assessments, it is important that we create appropriate alignment with the overarching curricular aim, most commonly referred to today as an academic content standard. For example, here is Standard RI.9–10.2 one of the English Language Arts Standards from the Common Core State Standards Initiative (National Governors Association Center for Best Practices and the Council of Chief State School Officers, 2010, p. 40): *Determine a central idea of a text and analyze its development over the course of the text, including how it emerges and is shaped and refined by specific details; provide an objective summary of the text.* One of the first orders of business is for the I-PLC team to determine the learning intentions inherent in such a broad curriculum goal. In the standard listed, the teachers might just focus on part of the overall goal in developing the initial learning intentions; that is, "*Determine a central idea of a text and analyze its development over the course of the text, including how it emerges and is shaped and refined by specific details.*" With that stated, a group of Language Arts teachers might surmise that students need to grasp three key pieces of enabling knowledge or skills in order to grasp this aim. For example, teachers might decide that the following are stepping-stones for reaching the lofty goal of just the first part of reaching mastery on this academic content standard:

1. Identify key details within an informational text.

2. Combine the key details of an informational text to determine the central idea.

3. Justify the selection of the central idea based on specific textual details from the text.

In the traditional use of formative assessment, it is common practice to use what has come to be known as a pretest/posttest model. That is the broad curricular aim is assessed at the beginning of an instructional cycle with a pretest. Once this evidence is obtained about what students know or do not know about the topic, in this example—determining the central idea of an informational text—then teachers prepare and plan to teach the unit usually for a period of approximately two to four weeks. After instruction, then teachers use a posttest to determine what students learned, or did not learn (see Figure 5.3).

In TFM, the recommendation is that formative analysis is an ongoing process that is used periodically throughout instruction at key points along the way, preferably after each key learning intention (see Figure 5.4).

Once I-PLCs determine the learning intentions for the most critical curricular aims or standards, formative assessment takes place after

Figure 5.3　Traditional Pretest/Posttest Model

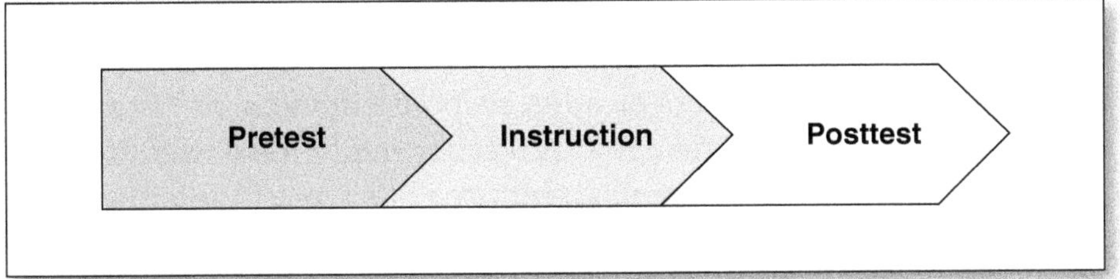

Figure 5.4　*The Focus Model* Formative Analysis Process

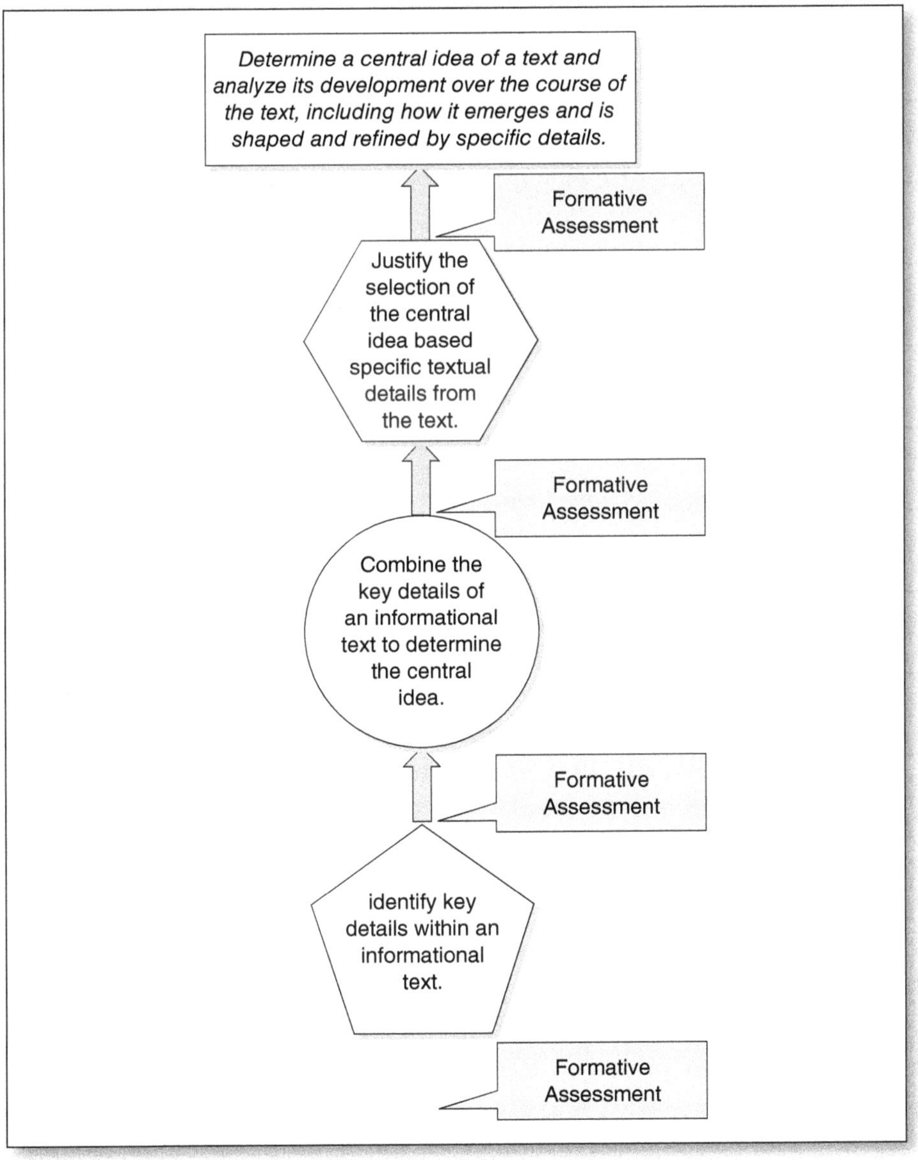

instruction on each of the learning intentions. Again, these are not haphazard decisions made in the heat of the moment. These are carefully planned and well thought out assessment gathering tasks that may take the form of pre-bells before class, scripted questions with the use of electronic clickers or other response devices, or "exit slips" at the end of class, to name a few. A teacher might have used these as informal assessments in the past, but in TFM we add intentionality and boost the impact on student achievement by being very specific about what we are measuring, why we are measuring, and what we intend to do with the results.

Therefore, when we create assessment items, we go directly back to the learning intentions. Thus, if we were constructing an assessment that covered the full range of the ELA standard previously described we plan assessment items that cause students to *determine the central idea of a text using particular details* and ask students to *construct a summary distinct from opinion or judgments*. Only with this intentional alignment can we have confidence that our assessments lead to valid inferences about student ability on the broader curricular aim. But this search is not just for the sake of gathering information about student learning, it is also about seeking information about the success of the teaching or the lack thereof. Only when teachers seek to know their effects on students can we hope to make instructional data-driven decisions based on evidence, which in turn results in a much higher probability of improved student results (Hattie, 2012).

Decisions, Decisions, Decisions

One more key point to consider before moving on to the types of items that we might include on a formative assessment, is that in Figure 5.4, for each formative assessment occurrence, teachers need to determine what "adjustment triggers" they need to set (Popham, 2008, p. 64). In other words, how many students are in the class, at what proficiency level and at what level should each individual student score to help teachers make the decision to either provide additional intervention (if students did not meet goal), or less intervention (if students met the goal in less time than expected). For example, in the author's school, teachers set an individual student proficiency rate of at least 80 percent mastery before moving to another step in the learning progression (learning intention). In addition, the overall class rate was set at 80 percent as well. So a typical decision point goal looks like this: In 10th-grade Language Arts, 80 percent or more of students need to score 80 percent or higher on the writing sample or we need to spend an additional two days, Friday and Monday, reviewing the key steps in organizing writing. This is an example of what Popham (2008) calls needing to make an *increase* instructional decision. This relates to the fact that teachers are setting in place, before the assessment ever takes place, a performance goal that dictates their future instructional actions. Now if students really bombed, the decision is not just that more instruction is needed, but certainly could be about the need for different instruction! On the flip side, if the previous goal is exceeded, and 95 percent of the kids score at the 94 percent level or higher, teachers can make a *decrease* instructional decision; that is instead of deciding to add additional time on the learning intention, teachers may actually move to the next learning intention more rapidly than they initially planned (Popham, 2008).

Selected Response Items

Many of the items that educators choose to use on assessments are what are termed *selected-response items;* that is, the student selects a response from a provided list. This may be in the form of multiple-choice, binary response (true/false, yes/no, etc.), fill-in-the-blank with the answers provided, and matching items.

Multiple-Choice Items

Multiple-choice items are the most popular of the selected-response items employed by educators on assessments of any kind. There are many reasons that multiple-choice items are a popular choice for assessments. Electronic scoring makes these items fairly easy to score, and multiple-choice tests can sample large amounts of content with minimal effort.

Multiple-choice items can also be written to varying levels of difficulty to help gather evidence on the range of student understanding. In high school, this author was fortunate to have an advanced math teacher named Ms. Adene Hurst. All her assessments were multiple choice with the three choices being "Yes," "No," and "Not Necessarily." Let me assure you, much to the chagrin of my classmates and myself these items assessed the cognitive and knowledge levels at all dimensions. In addition, when written with intentionality, even the distractors (the answer choices other than the "best" answer choice) can provide evidence of student understanding, which can lead to inferences about student strengths and weaknesses within content. In many cases, if well written, we can learn as much or more from student responses that are "incorrect" as we can from those that are correct. All these reasons make multiple-choice items highly attractive and informative when written effectively.

On the other hand, poorly written multiple-choice items leave quite a bit to be desired. Sometimes, novices to assessment may include unintentional clues within the items that lead educators to make incorrect inferences about student ability. For example, if an educator depended on the following example, he or she could draw an invalid inference about student understanding of the targeted topic:

Choose the "best" answer for this statement.

1. The following is the method used by scientists to investigate problems:

    a. Coriolis effect

    b. Scientific method

    c. $E = mc^2$

    d. First law of thermodynamics

It would not take Einstein to determine that the use of the term *method* in the question stem is a blatant clue to the only "method" listed in the answer choices. Additionally, if not prepared carefully, multiple-choice items can solicit responses that only reach the remember-and-understand level and not the cognitive levels required to push students to the goals of many of the standards for which they are responsible. According to assessment expert James Popham (2003), "multiple-choice items can never measure a student's ability to creatively synthesize content of any sort" (p. 82). This is why we should seek a balance between the types of items we include on any assessment.

Thomas Haladyna and Steven Downing (1989) conducted an in-depth review of the more than 40 sources of guidelines for writing effective test items and used it to develop what has been termed a *taxonomy of multiple-choice item writing rules.* When 70 percent or more of the authors within these sources agreed on a particular rule, it was considered to have "validity by consensus" (Haladyna & Downing, 1989, p. 37). Of the 46 rules identified, the following 13 had the highest incidence of agreement:

1. Use only plausible distractors—93 percent agreement

2. Question/completion format—89 percent agreement

3. Emphasize higher level thinking—85 percent agreement

4. Keep option lengths similar—83 percent agreement

5. Balance the key—83 percent agreement

6. Avoid grammatical clues—80 percent agreement

7. Avoid clues to the right answer—78 percent agreement

8. Avoid negative stems—76 percent agreement

9. Use only one correct option—76 percent agreement

10. Give clear directions—74 percent agreement

11. Include main idea in stem—74 percent agreement

12. Avoid "all of the above"—74 percent agreement

13. Avoid "none of the above"—72 percent agreement

List adapted from Haladyna and Downing (1989, p. 46).

The authors found that these 13 rules had the most support from the literature, indicating that they had the least disagreement on their importance. Thus, the consensus is that these rules are the universally accepted best practice when it comes to building effective multiple-choice test items.

Using Plausible Distractors

If properly designed, the key to the use of critical formative analysis is that we learn just as much from the evidence collected when students are able to choose the one "best" answer as we do when they choose one of the distractors. This is why it is important to stress the quality of the items written in place of simple quantity. The choice of either answer by the testee provides information to make an inference. For example, using the example in Table 5.5, what does each distractor tell us about the student?

What process is most nearly the opposite of photosynthesis?

Each distractor provides for a specific inference to student understanding of the topic under assessment. Through practice and feedback and in order to help us gain more evidence about student strengths and obstacles to learning, we can learn to write items with a more specific ability to provide inferences related to the understanding of algorithms in math, and so on.

When it comes to the number and types of items to include on assessments, there is no hard-and-fast rule. The recommendation of TFM for any general assessment is a ratio of roughly 80 percent

Table 5.5 Distractor Analysis

Possible Inference	
Distractor	A. Digestion—At a much more macro-level than photosynthesis.
Distractor	B. Relaxation—Process more readily associated with muscle contraction.
Correct Answer	C. *Respiration*—Student has correctly identified the opposite process.
Distractor	D. Exertion—Opposite of B, more associated with muscle contraction.

selected response items to 20 percent constructed response items. Inherent in the decision to select item types is that the purpose of the assessment should drive the item type used. For example, an assessment of the ability to generate a type of writing may consist of only a single constructed response writing prompt. These are all important considerations for the use of any selected response type of question.

Binary Choice Items

Another common assessment type requires test takers to choose between only two options—thus, the name *binary* item. These items most commonly take the form of either true/false or yes/no items. They share some of the same advantages of the multiple-choice items—they can be used to sample large amounts of content while also allowing the educator some glimpse into student understanding. These items can also be written to higher levels of rigor when intentionally written.

A major negative when teachers rely on these types of items as the only type of item on the assessment, is that it can lead to the unenviable rote memorization of isolated facts (Popham, 2003, 2014). This reliance on surface-level understanding does not produce students who want to delve deeper into the conceptual and metacognitive dimensions; it also does not provide educators the proper evidence to make valid inferences on whether students have gone deeper in their learning (Hattie, 2012).

Some of the most commonly held rules for building effective binary choice items include the following:

1. Avoid statements that are too general.

2. Do not use negatives or double negatives.

3. Do not use long, complex sentences.

4. Do not include more than one idea.

5. If you are using an opinion, indicate the source.

6. True–false statements should be the same length.

7. Include the same number of true and false statements.

8. Do not use specific qualifiers, such as *always, never, all, none, usually, sometimes, occasionally, may,* or *could.*

List adapted from Michigan State University (MSU, 2009).

Finally, when it comes to creating effective binary choice items, James Popham (2003) recommends writing the items in pairs, then ideally if the item is a well thought-out stem, it can be stated in either the positive or negative. Here is an example:

T F An amendment to the Constitution requires a two-thirds majority of the states to approve the measure.

T F An amendment to the Constitution requires a simple majority of states to approve the measure.

As illustrated, the first item is entirely "true," and the second item is entirely "false." Only one item might be included on this assessment, but educators have another item to add to the item bank for the next assessment on this topic.

Multiple Binary Choice Items

One unique item type appears to be a cross between a multiple-choice item and a binary choice item. It is called a multiple binary choice item. The item consists of a stem followed by a cluster of binary items. These items can be true–false, right–wrong, yes–no, or any other type of binary choice. W. J. Popham (2014) speaks to the utility of these items and shares how he uses them in his graduate statistics class at the University of California, Los Angeles (UCLA). This type of item can be used to sample a fairly broad scope of content at a fairly high level of cognitive rigor. The benefits of these items are that they are (1) highly efficient at sampling content, (2) often more reliable that other types of selected response items, (3) in many ways like multiple-choice items in their ability to measure higher levels of cognitive knowledge and skills, and (4) perceived by test takers to be more difficult than multiple-choice items (Popham, 2014). Note the following example:

Utilize the following text to determine if the statements that follow are correct or incorrect. Circle [C] for correct and [IC] for incorrect in regard to the numbered statement. Each item is worth 2 points.

- *We the People of the United States, in Order to form a more perfect Union, establish Justice, insure domestic Tranquility, provide for the common defense, promote the general Welfare, and secure the Blessings of Liberty to ourselves and our Posterity, do ordain and establish this Constitution for the United States of America.* (constitutionus.com, 2014)

1. This preamble is used to overview the basic rights afforded by the constitution . . .   C   IC

2. The preamble contains no reference to the government responsibility of providing national defense . . .   C   IC

3. Three specific responsibilities of the federal government spelled out in the preamble are the promotion of the general welfare, justice, and the insurance of domestic tranquility . . . C   IC

Popham (2014) and Frisbie (1992) make some key recommendations about developing multiple binary choice–type items. First, make certain to separate the clusters of binary items clearly from sets that might be linked to a different stimulus or prompt. In addition, it is important that the cluster of items relate homogenously to the stem. Last, if test developers intend to use more than one of these items, then it is very important that some formatting is done to ensure that test takers can determine where the stimulus material begins and the clusters of items ends. This can be a major source of confusion if not handled appropriately. In the previous example, the dotted lines were used to make sure that students could determine where one item begins and another ends.

Matching Items

The assessment type commonly used by educators to measure the students' ability to connect multiple sources of knowledge when names, dates, places, and events are important is the matching item. The typical matching item consists of two columns containing a list of stems or premises, and a column containing a list of responses (Clay, 2001; Haladyna & Downing, 1989; Popham, 2003, 2014).

Matching items have this element in common with the multiple-choice and binary items: the strength of covering large amounts of content as long as associations exist between the stems and the responses.

This can be highly desirable in the subject areas of history, social studies, and science, especially when the learning intention calls for students to be able to show a surface-level understanding of the relationship between the stems and responses. Unfortunately, this level of cognitive demand is most frequently at the knowledge level. The limited cognitive load placed on students by the matching item is the major disadvantage of these types of items. Matching items are primarily designed to determine student understanding regarding groups of related ideas. This convention prevents them from providing sufficient evidence to formulate valid inferences on more specific singular details, which requires the use of other item types on the assessment to be more specific about student understanding and ability.

Some commonly held rules for writing effective matching items are the following:

1. Include homogeneous material in each set of items.

2. Include at least 3 to 5 but no more than 8 to 10 items in a matching set.

3. Be careful to eliminate irrelevant clues.

4. Place each set of matching items on a single page.

5. Compose the response list of single words or very short phrases.

6. Arrange the responses in systematic order: alphabetical, chronological, and so on.

7. Do not have the same number of items and options.

8. Be clear in the directions about how items are to be matched and the number of times responses might be used (i.e., more than once, only once, etc.)

List adapted from Haladyna and Downing (1989); MSU (2009); and Popham (2003, 2014).

An example of a matching item set might look like the following:

Directions: On the line to the left of each cell function in Column I in Table 5.6, write the letter of the cell organelle from the list in Column II that serves that function within an animal cell. Each organelle name may be used only one time.

As was mentioned earlier, this format only gives us a ballpark understanding that students have a cursory remembrance of how

Table 5.6

Column I: Cell Functions	Column II: Cell Organelles
_____1. Serves as the cell transport system	A. Nucleus
_____2. Directs the activities of the cell	B. Vacuole
_____3. Stores water and other substances in the cell	C. Mitochondria
_____4. Separates the cell from the environment	D. Cell Membrane
	E. Endoplasmic Reticulum

these various organelles operate within the cell. We need to delve deeper with other items if we want to make inferences about students' true understandings of what any of these organelles' more specific functions are within the cell. We can certainly probe deeper using other types of items on the assessment.

Constructed Response Items

To delve more deeply into student understanding on assessments, educators can choose to have students construct their response in lieu of selecting it from a provided list of options. In many cases, when students generate original responses to questions it ups the level of complexity of the item. Many times, these items are written to require students to analyze and evaluate and thus create a response in reaction to the stimulus or prompt. Popham (2003) stated, "Because a student really needs to understand something to be able to construct a response based on that understanding, in many instances (but not all), students' responses to these sorts of items will better contribute to more valid inferences . . ." (p. 87).

For students to be successful on effective constructed response items, the required understanding or the depth of knowledge at the conceptual level, and in some cases the metacognitive level, lends itself to the power that requiring nonfiction informative writing can have as an instructional tool. Writing helps students organize their thinking and make their understanding more visible to themselves and the teacher. According to Robert Marzano (2012), "The logic behind the assumption that writing should be integral to instruction in all subject areas is that writing is fundamentally a constructive process of encoding new information" (p. 82). Researcher Doug Reeves has also been a long-time proponent of the positive impact that requiring student writing can have on achievement. According to Reeves (2010a), "There are no silver bullets in education. But writing—particularly nonfiction writing—is about as close as you can get to a single strategy that has significant and positive effects in nearly every other area of the curriculum" (p. 46).

This act of students laying bare the depth of their understanding also produces more evidence that teachers can use to make valid inferences about student understanding. In addition, having students construct their responses can help teachers more readily and efficiently identify strengths and weaknesses. Thus, writing can not only be a powerful assessment tool, but the process of writing can also be a high-yield instructional strategy used to help students deepen their thinking to the conceptual dimension and beyond.

The primary disadvantage to using constructed response items are that they can be cumbersome to score depending on their length. This process can be made more efficient with the development of an effective scoring guide or rubric. With practice, teachers and students can become very adept at using rubrics to make the scoring of longer constructed response items more effective and efficient. Ideally, good scoring guides are used as instructional tools and are given to students as a part of effective classroom instruction so that they can use the success criteria contained with the rubric to meet the expectations of the standards.

Some of the most crucial constructed response items should be the essential questions derived from the broader curricular aims or even some of the beefier learning intentions (Wiggins & McTighe, 1998, 2013). The rubric is then built around the success criteria that teachers collaboratively develop that are directly aligned to the learning intentions before instruction ever begins. This ensures that instruction, assessment, and standards are seamlessly aligned throughout the instructional process. The collaboration needed to effectively guide this process takes place within the structure of the I-PLCs at the system, school, and classroom levels. Constructing effective scoring guides is an essential part of building effective constructed response items.

Short Constructed Response Items

A common form of constructed response item that lessens the burden of scoring an extended essay is the short constructed response item. These items can typically be answered with a single word or as few as one to three sentences. Short answer items allow for the sampling of rather robust amounts of content and are fairly easy to score. Teachers can vary the expectations of the item and can in turn change the amount of time required to complete the assessment items. It takes considerably less time for students to supply the term than to write out the definitions to a set of vocabulary. Teachers can vary what is required of students to modulate the time mandated for short constructed response items.

A disadvantage to this type of assessment item is that less input is required from the students in an attempt to save on time, which can lead to rote memorization and lower cognitive complexity. Finally, it is critical that teachers use effective instruction to set the expectation for the answers desired on the assessment. Again, having instruction, assessment, and standards aligned through the Uncovering the Standards process goes a long way to eliminate the ambiguity that can creep into constructed response items.

Some important considerations for writing effective short constructed response items include the following:

1. Use direct questions rather than incomplete statements.

2. Structure items so that they necessitate brief, distinctive responses.

3. For incomplete statement type questions, restrict the number of blanks to one or, at most, two.

4. Place the blank near the end of an incomplete sentence or in the margin for a direct question.

5. Blanks for answers should be equal in length.

6. Provide sufficient answer space.

List adapted from Haladyna and Downing (1989); and Popham (2003, 2014).

Extended Constructed Response

Depending on the purpose of the assessment, which should be aligned to the broader curricular aim and learning intentions, teachers may seek an extended response from students in the form of a single paragraph, multiple paragraphs, or an essay. These items are referred to as *extended constructed response items*. Essay or extended constructed response items are very effective when the goal is to measure sophisticated dimensions of student knowledge. In addition, extended constructed response items also give teachers a glimpse into the depth of student understanding, which typically is not provided in other assessment types. This can make it easier for teachers to diagnose strengths and weaknesses in understanding and make for better inferences about what students comprehend.

The three major disadvantages to using this type of item on assessments are the time required to score the items, the scope of content that might be covered, and the subjectivity that can sneak into the scoring of such items. All three of these areas of concern can be addressed with proper construction of the item itself. Clarity in the directions provided to students about what are the expectations for the item, the alignment of the scoring guide or rubric used to judge the correctness of the response to the standard, and thus, the directions provided to students can all work in concert to make for an effective assessment task that has the potential to allow for valid inferences to be made about student status.

General writing guidelines for extended constructed-response items include the following:

1. Make sure to structure items so that the task required of students is very specific.

2. For each item, make sure to communicate the expected response length, the point-value for the correct response, and even the amount of time that should be allotted to the response.

3. As a good rule of thumb, include multiple questions that require shorter responses and fewer questions demanding lengthy answers.

4. Do not employ optional questions.

5. Verify a question's quality by writing a trial response to the question.

6. Prior to reviewing examinee responses, prepare a tentative scoring key.

7. Score all answers to one question before scoring the next question.

8. Make prior decisions regarding treatment of factors, such as spelling and punctuation.

9. Evaluate essay responses anonymously.

List adapted from Haladyna and Downing (1989); and Popham (2003, 2014).

Any effective use of extended constructed response greatly depends on the creation of the rubric or scoring guide that defines the success criteria for the task. This rubric should be directly aligned to the broader curricular aim and learning intentions and clearly articulated in the directions for the task so that students successfully comprehend the expectations for performance.

Creating Effective Scoring Guides

John Hattie (2012) found that of the 150 different innovations he studied that impact on student achievement, the number one influence from the contribution of students on achievement was what he termed "Self-Reported Grades" (p. 43). According to the research, spanning more than 900 meta-analyses and taking into account more than 250 million students, self-reported grades had the highest effect size (effect size d = 1.44). As the average effect size of all variables impacting student achievement was d = .40, we see that the highest effect size variable of self-reported grades has an impact 360 percent larger than the average effect. Very simply, the idea of self-reported grades is that students understand the learning intentions and the success criteria so well that they are able to self-assess where their performance measures in relation to these criteria, and furthermore, they are able to articulate specific next steps that they as students need to take to reach the learning goal. In other words, the students become self-regulated in their learning (Hattie, 2009, 2012).

This is not to say that teachers take a passive role in the learning or teaching process. On the contrary, Hattie (2009, 2012) strongly pointed to the fact that this level of understanding requires vast amounts of direct instruction on the part of the teacher using the effective tools of scoring guides, clearly articulated learning intentions with success criteria, and a constant stream of specific, timely, and task-oriented feedback. Often, feedback takes the form of positive or negative affirmation or self-affirmation (e.g., Good Job, Excellent, etc.). The most effective feedback is directly related to the learning task (e.g., you really seem to have a grasp of the order of operations as apparent by your success on this problem set). Not that positive affirmation is a bad thing; it just does not pass the test as being most effective when it comes to providing students clear, concise, and effective comments that can help to deepen their learning and academic confidence.

One major influence on a student's ability to self-regulate in learning is the teacher's expression of elevated expectations for that student. Hattie found that one of the most limiting factors in student achievement was the expectation of teachers and students of the students' ability. Hattie's research showed this to be especially self-limiting for minority and lower achieving students. The use of a standards-based curriculum, with a rigorous objective criterion for success (clear learning intentions and success criteria) that is clearly articulated to students through TFM is the starting point for creating equity in the classroom and expectations. The culmination then is the development of an aligned scoring guide or rubric that clearly articulates to all students what they need to know and be able to do to achieve proficiency on the success criteria articulated from the standard. Thus, creating effective scoring guides is about much more than simply creating more effective assessment items. More important, it is about bringing to life the equity that all students deserve in every class, providing the effective feedback that all students need to engage in learning, and fostering the drive for self-regulated learning within students; all of which can truly transform student circumstances and lives.

Building effective scoring guides takes us back to the process of creating learning intentions. From the learning intention, we first determine what it means for a student to be proficient on the learning intention by developing the success criteria. This becomes our criteria for the "proficient" designation in our scoring guide. To create the other three points within our rubric, we simply embellish the criteria for proficient work indicating the deeper understanding we expect if want to label the work as "exemplary." In the other direction of the rubric, if a student does not meet all the criteria for proficiency (e.g., completes 2 out of 3), the student is labelled as "progressing." Finally, if the student meets less than the criteria for progressing, we indicate that the student needs to "retry" after additional instruction. The rubric just described looks something like this:

Language Arts

Determine a central idea of a text and how it is conveyed through particular details; provide a summary of the text distinct from personal opinions or judgments. (RI.6.2 [CCSS ELA, 2010, para. 39])

Learning Intentions

- Identify key details within a text.
- Determine the central idea of a text.
- Analyze a text and provide an objective summary.

Success Criteria

- Using a highlighter, identify the key details in an informational text.
- Write an expository paragraph identifying the central idea of an informational text.
- Create a summary of an informational text that is free of personal opinion and judgments.

Assessment Task Directions

Using the sample text provided, **write a paragraph identifying the central idea of a text** and how it is conveyed through particular details; be sure to **provide at least 3 details** supporting this idea as central to the text. In addition, **provide a one paragraph summary of the text distinct from personal opinions or judgments.** This item counts for 20 percent of the assessment score, and you should allot no more than 20 minutes for this exercise.

Rubric

The strength in writing the rubric with this primary focus on what it means to be "proficient" is that it maintains the focus of students and teachers, keeping the goal of proficiency at the forefront. Regardless of where the student currently falls within the rubric, by meeting the success criteria that are clearly articulated within the rubric, not only are they successful on the task or assessment, but also because the rubric is directly aligned to the standards, there is also ideally some predictive value toward the broader curricular aim defined by the academic content standard.

In Table 5.7, also notice that the proficient criteria are clearly articulated in the directions for the assessment task. This is accomplished by simply going to the standard and using the learning intentions and success criteria to clearly state for students what they are expected to know and do. This takes the mystery out of learning. Larry Ainsworth observed that after a group of teachers actually engaged students in helping refine the rubrics created for a class, "they [the students] were noticeably more motivated than usual, and better prepared to actually produce the corresponding quality work because they understood what was expected" (Ainsworth & Viegut, 2006, p. 85). Rubrics should certainly be an integral part of instruction and assessment and should be the tools that teachers use to help students move toward self-regulation.

Table 5.7 Scoring Guide/Rubric for Constructed Response

Exemplary *The student:*	*Proficient* *The student:*	*Progressing* *The student:*	*Retry after additional instruction* *The student:*
In addition to the proficient criteria: Is able to compare and contrast the central idea of this text with one of the previous texts discussed in this class.	In addition to the progressing criteria: Is able to write a paragraph identifying the central idea of a text. **Provide at least 3 details** supporting this idea as central to the text. Provide a one paragraph summary of the text distinct from personal opinions or judgments.	Effectively completes two of the three proficient criteria. All sentences are grammatically correct and paragraphs are effectively written as defined by our class criteria.	Effectively completes less than two of the three proficient criteria. Sentences are not grammatically correct and/or paragraphs are not written as defined by our class criteria.

Rubrics provide an excellent vehicle to help students develop the ability to answer the three most important questions regarding feedback found in the *Visible Learning* research by John Hattie (2009, p. 37):

1. Where am I going?

2. How am I going?

3. Where to next?

The answers we hope students grasp are the following:

Answer to Question 1: ***Mastery of the learning intentions!***

Answer to Question 2: ***Formative analysis (formative assessment), which provides the information students need to gauge where they are currently in relation to the success criteria (proficiency).***

Answer to Question 3: ***By receiving timely, actionable, and specific feedback, students can use this information to make adjustments to learning tactics and work thereby demonstrating proficiency or going beyond proficiency to the exemplary level.***

Used effectively, scoring guides have the potential to foster success for students on gaining proficiency on the learning intentions, success on aligned classroom tasks, and success on assessments aligned to the broader curricular aims as well.

Other Tools to Gather Evidence

In addition to the traditional paper and pencil assessments, performance assessments can also be used to gather information to help formulate inferences. According to Popham (2014), performance assessments are an assessment approach that seeks to determine student status on educational variables of interest by observing the way that students complete a single task or a series of tasks. Once teachers identify a priority curricular aim worthy of the time and planning needed to implement such an assessment, they then work to develop a single task or a series of tasks, which by the very nature of their completion provide legitimate evidence regarding a student's abilities with an important skill or understanding. These tasks can be designed using the taxonomy of choice, whether Bloom's (2001), Webb's (1997) DOK, or the SOLO taxonomy introduced earlier in Chapter 3.

Important considerations for these types of assessments are that ideally they provide a connection with real-world significance for students, they are genuinely demanding, and ideally the skills required have generalizability outside of the specific tasks in the assessment. The goal is to develop skills through the course of the engagement in the task or tasks within the performance assessment that will prove beneficial long after the assessment is over.

As previously reviewed, let's use a language arts class studying the following standard:

Language Arts

Determine a central idea of a text and how it is conveyed through particular details; provide a summary of the text distinct from personal opinions or judgments. (RI.6.2 [CCSS ELA, 2010, p. 39])

Learning Intentions

- Identify key details within a text.
- Determine the central idea of a text.
- Analyze a text and provide an objective summary.

Success Criteria

- Using a highlighter, identify the key details in an informational text.
- Write an expository paragraph identifying the central idea of an informational text.
- Create a summary of an informational text that is free of personal opinion and judgments.

Now, teachers simply design one to four performance tasks increasing in cognitive complexity from lower levels to a culminating activity that should stretch students to the highest levels of cognitive challenge depicted in the broader curricular aim and learning intentions. We can scaffold these tasks so that students gain the surface-level knowledge needed to develop the deeper conceptual and metacognitive knowledge necessary for success on the more cognitively demanding requirements of the standard. For example, the following four performance tasks were created to produce an engaging foundation for instruction using the sample standards around the scenario in Table 5.8.

In this simplified example of the performance assessment design process, as the tasks progress, they get more and more cognitively demanding. In addition, the tasks are tightly aligned to the broad academic content standard and the learning intentions.

In a real case for a unit of study, there are usually two or more academic content standards and their learning intentions that are

Table 5.8   Sample Scaffolded Performance Tasks

Task 1	Task 2	Task 3	Task 4
Read the provided informational text, identify the key details using a graphic representation.	Combine the key details in the informational text that you read into the central idea for this informational text. Describe how this central idea is developed across the text by the details used by the author.	Create an explanatory essay describing a justification for your selection of the main idea. Compare and contrast the main idea of this piece of text to at least one other work we read this week.	Create a summary of an informational text that is free of personal opinion and judgments. In addition to the summary, create a paragraph theorizing how the central idea changes if one or more of the key details you select is not present.

the focus; therefore, the tasks necessarily are elaborate to incorporate more of the knowledge and skills from the standards and learning intentions within the unit. Last, to make sure that the success criteria are clear for all, a scoring guide is developed for each individual task.

Three Important Classroom Assessment Considerations

According to education assessment expert James Popham (2013), "validity is the cornerstone of educational assessment" (p. 18). Many times we seek to give the inanimate object (i.e., the test or assessment), the character of validity. In truth, when determining the validity of an assessment, we are really referring to the validity of the test-based inference we make using the evidence from the assessment of a student's overt performance in relationship to some covert variable.

Assessment experts consider three types of validity in relation to the evidence gathered from assessments: content-related, criterion-related, and construct-related (Popham, 2013, 2014). Of the three types, content-related evidence of validity is most directly aligned to our discussion in this book specific to effective formative assessment practices. Content-related validity simply relates to the amount of evidence that exists supporting the fact that assessment items actually measure the critical learning targets or curricular aims that the assessment was intended to measure. This is essential if educators are to rely on the evidence from the assessment to make inferences that are valid. The quality of these inferences invariably has an overwhelming impact on the quality of the instructional decisions that are made as a result of these inferences as well. The cornerstone of effective formative assessment is the use of assessments that lead to valid evidence-based inferences.

Content-related evidence can be obtained in the context of the use of the I-PLC structure discussed in Chapter 7. Collaboratively, teachers look at all assessment items while using the graphic organizer containing the academic content standard, the learning intentions, and the success criteria. By using this committee approach, teachers can determine if the assessment item truly measures the intended outcomes, and using the previously discussed taxonomies, determine if the item has the same expectation of rigor as the parent academic content standard. (In addition, remember also to consider using the SOLO taxonomy to measure the level of thinking of the response provided by the student.) This process is parallel to the procedures that assessment item writers use for standardized tests. Yet again, this is just one more reason why the collaborative structure of the I-PLCs proves itself as a powerful strategy to help improve student achievement and the effectiveness of instructional decisions.

Finally, one more area for review when it comes to creating assessments that provides the ability for teachers to make more valid inferences is the variable of assessment bias; namely, to eliminate those items from the assessment that might offend or punish a student because of demographic factors (gender, race, ethnicity) or other defining group characteristics, such as socioeconomic status (SES) or religion. Standardized tests are notorious for using items related to SES to get the score spread required for normative comparisons (Popham, 2014). This practice clouds the evidence gathered by assessments and thus leads to invalid inferences. In the end, this procedure can lead teachers to make instructional decisions based on faulty information. The following is an example of an SES-related faux pas:

My mother's field is court reporting.

Choose the sentence below in which the word *field* means the same as it does in the boxed sentence above.

A. The first baseman knew how to field his position.

B. Farmer Jones added fertilizer to his field.

C. What field will you enter after school is complete?

D. The doctor checked my field of vision. (Popham, 2012, p. 24)

According to expert James Popham, students from socioeconomically disadvantaged backgrounds are less likely to refer to their parent's occupations as *fields*. This nuance can certainly lead to this item eliciting invalid evidence based on bias. This variable can be avoided or held in check by using a similar procedure as prescribed when preparing validity reviews with a panel of colleagues. Again, the context of the I-PLC delivers the perfect structure to perform a review of the items related to assessment bias. It is vital to ensure that student responses to assessment items give us a clear picture about student understanding of the learning intention rather than to some variable not related to the evidence we seek. I-PLCs are sensitive to review assessments for both content-related evidence of validity and for assessment bias in order to ensure that the assessments give us a true picture of student status of student knowledge and understanding.

Formative Analysis Process

In this chapter, a great deal of time has been spent on the finer points of effective assessment. The real power comes from what we actually do with the information we gain from the assessment. This is directly related to what Steven White (2011) calls "going beyond the numbers" (p. 10). The idea of using this information also goes directly to the heart of effective accountability. As Dr. White put it,

> Accountability is the authority to commit resources (*to take action*), responsibility to demonstrate improvement (*results*), and permission to adjust time and opportunity (*permission to subtract*) so that all students achieve beyond their expectations and the expectations of adults committed to their achievement (parents, teachers, other educators). (2011, p. 80)

Going beyond simply collecting the data is what formative analysis is all about. In the next chapter, we discuss the vehicle that we use at the system, school, and, most importantly, at the classroom level to carry out this systematic approach through the use of I-PLCs. Only through using structured educator collaboration focused on teaching and learning can we hope to reach our full potential as educators and, along with our students, as learners. I-PLCs answer the question, "Okay, we got data—now what?"

KEY CONSIDERATIONS

Formative analysis is more than simply assessing or testing students. As a tool, formative assessment has been used so loosely by so many for so long that we have yet to recognize the full potential of this high-powered instructionally embedded assessment process that many researchers found can literally double the rate of student learning. When educators and students use assessment in real time to grow student and teacher knowledge, and deepen understanding by the high-quality feedback that such rich assessment provides, the sky is the limit. Formative analysis is more comprehensive than the common pre- and posttest models that many educators implemented in their efforts to harness the power of formative assessment. The true use of formative assessment represents a culture change at the classroom, the school, and the system level.

Guiding Questions

1. Why do teachers in your school or district assess?

2. Of the data from assessments that you collect in your school or district, can you point to specific ways that you use these data to improve teaching and learning? What is the evidence?

3. What types of feedback do teachers provide students in your school or district? How do students provide feedback to teachers? How is this feedback driven by clear success criteria related to learning intentions?

4. How do teachers provide task-oriented feedback to students based on assessment results?

5. How do you describe the level of student engagement in instruction within your school or district? What real-life learning connections are available for students?

6. How does the information from assessments drive the modification of teacher strategies and student learning tactics within your classroom, school, or district?

6

Collaboration

Alone we can do so little; together we can do so much.

Helen Keller

Collaboration: Why Is it Counterintuitive?

Why do educators collaborate? Because they are placed around a table and have data, right? Well, just as one television commentator is fond of saying, "Not so fast, my friend!" Even with the buzz today about the need for effective collaboration, why is it that schools continue to struggle with their quest to establish effective teacher teams that can lead to improved instructional decisions, and translate into improved student results? In the world of education, collaboration does not just happen; it is preceded by structure, planning, and groundwork. In addition, the need for continued support and monitoring is vital. If effective collaboration is going to succeed, it is essential that part of the duties of the many instructional leaders at the system and the school level are related to fostering, nurturing, and supporting these structures. According to Troen and Boles (2012), principals are the "unsung key players in team development" (p. 8). The fact is that because true collaboration runs counter to the traditional culture of schooling, it takes distributed leadership from the system to classroom level to develop teams that talk the talk and walk the walk of getting to the heart of analyzing evidence and making real-time decisions about improving teaching and learning.

This portrait of schooling and education is completely at odds with the 150-year-old prototypical model for schools that paralleled the industrial model of disconnected workers working on an assembly line. On a recent plane trip, this author had a discussion with a prominent former governor who shared this observation: He thought that if his dad, who died in 1950, came back to life today, one of the areas that his dad could visit that had changed very little since the year of his death would be a classroom in a typical school. Just to reiterate that point, you can make the statement that a typical classroom has changed very little not just since 1950, but also in more than 100 years. Most troubling is that the preponderance of evidence on effective schooling shouts out to us: To make the best educational decisions, we must use effective collaborative structures, make decisions founded on real-time evidence and based on a prioritized set of learning targets. This is the rationale for the focus model of school improvement.

Support for Collaboration

One of the many organizations that support effective learning communities or effective collaboration is Learning Forward, also known as The Professional Learning Association. Learning Forward (2013) defines *learning communities* as follows:

> Learning Communities: Professional learning that increases educator effectiveness and results for all students occurs within learning communities committed to continuous improvement, collective responsibility, and goal alignment.

There is no better representation of this expectation than TFM. As we see in the next chapter, the culmination of TFM is a collaborative structure grounded in goals set for the long-, mid-, and short-term that drive the process of continuous improvement and are rooted in the idea of collective responsibility for the solution and results.

Learning Forward (2013) defines *continuous improvement* through the following characteristics:

A. The use of data to determine student and educator learning needs;

B. Identification of shared goals for student and educator learning;

C. Professional learning to extend educators' knowledge of content, content-specific pedagogy, how students learn, and management of classroom environments;

D. Selection and implementation of appropriate evidence-based strategies to achieve student and educator learning goals;

E. Application of the learning with local support at the work site;

F. Use of evidence to monitor and refine implementation; and

G. Evaluation of results.

Each step of the I-PLC process addresses each of these characteristics. Real-time data elicited from formative assessment is used to set goals for students and teachers in the implementation of effective instructional strategies targeted at identified students needs. In addition, the students are also able to use this evidence to make adjustments as needed to their learning tactics and set individual goals related to continuous improvement and responsibility for their learning. The entire process is grounded in both teachers and students taking a problem-solving approach to teaching and learning. The goals are that students to become more self-regulated in their learning and that teachers are better able to determine the impact of their teaching based on the results seen within the students. This evaluation of both the strategies employed by the teacher and the student is ultimately measured by the impact of those strategies on student results. Each characteristic within the continuous improvement framework is inherent in each step of the I-PLC process and the overall focus model for school improvement.

Collective Responsibility

Another important caveat is the idea of collective responsibility. The I-PLC process provides the structure where educators are concerned with not just the learning of their particular sample of students, but *ALL* students within the content area or grade level served by the team. Thus, the members of the team then take collective responsibility for the learning of all students within the school. In addition to taking collective responsibility for the learning of students, teams also take on the responsibility for the development of each team members' instructional capacity. Through a process similar to that described in *Instructional Rounds in Education* by City, Elmore, Fiarman, and Teital (2010) and in *"Kaizen"* (Toyota, n.d.), teams set about the business of taking collective responsibility for improving the instructional process. Conclusively, teachers and students take on collective responsibility for the learning as students are engaged in setting goals and using assessment evidence to make adjustments in learning tactics as well.

Structure for Collaboration

In addition to the four core practices explicit in TFM that we discuss throughout this book, the previous references, *Instructional Rounds* and *Kaizen* are very much a part of the reflective work that is essentially a part of an effective teacher team. Instructional Rounds is an observation process that was derived from the model of medical rounds adopted by many physicians in honing and developing their professional practice. City et al. (2010) chronicled this process in their book *Instructional Rounds in Education*. Ultimately, members of the observation team identify a predetermined "problem of practice," formulate some strategies related to addressing the identified problem, and through direct observation, feedback, and deliberate practice on implementation, take the learning and the application to the next level to solve or address the problem of practice and thus improve the teaching. This deep reflective focus on instructional practice translates into improved student results when the problem of practice chosen is directly related to student needs, teacher needs, or obstacles to learning.

The other reflective process, *Kaizen*, is a Japanese business philosophy of continuous improvement. This process can and has been applied to the process of schooling through focusing on the improvement of teaching, sometimes referred to as lesson study. This philosophy is counter to the idea "if it's not broken, don't fix it." *Kaizen* holds that no process is ever perfect, thus improvement is an ongoing process. According to a company that practices *kaizen*, the automaker Toyota (n.d.) describes the philosophy this way:

> Kaizen in practice means that all team members in all parts of the organization are continuously looking for ways to improve operations, and people at every level in the company support this process of improvement.
>
> Kaizen also requires the setting of clear objectives and targets. It is very much a matter of positive attitude, with the focus on what *should* be done rather than what *can* be done. ("About Us," paragraphs 2 and 3)

In addition to this idea of continuous improvement, Toyota takes the process a step further by employing three filters that ensure that this continuous improvement is vetted in such a way that it truly leads to helpful innovation, and not simply superfluous activity. These filters are part of what is called the TPS system, which incorporates the "5 whys" and the "5S concept."

The TPS, the Toyota Production System or Thinking People System holds that people need to be constantly thinking and reflecting on the work of the team and how this work can be improved. Team members can and should not act like robots. The belief is that the process of giving people the task of making real-time decisions to help improve the organization helps build efficacy of the individual and thus feeds into the collective efficacy of the organization. According to Toyota (2013), "Kaizen is not just based on improvements being developed and implemented only by experts or management. It involves everybody, relying on the extensive knowledge, skills and experience of the people working directly in the process" (para. 2). This is truly at the heart of effective teacher teams. Effective schools do not make decisions in a top-down manner. It takes all within the schools focused on the core work of teaching and learning to help make the decisions required to improve the instructional core.

The "5 whys" process is used to test the logic of a proposed innovation or change. At Toyota (2013), any new recommended change must, "be tested by questioning 'why?' at five levels to ensure that its logic and value is clear" (5 whys, para. 2). When evaluating effective teacher teaming, the classroom is at the ground level to look at evidence of student learning and to assess student strengths and obstacles to learning in relation to particular critical learning targets. The *whys* of concern for the effective teacher team are the following:

1. Why is a focus on this particular knowledge or skill critical for student success in college and career, the next level of learning, or on high stakes assessments?

2. Why is this an obstacle to student learning?

3. Why is this strategy the best one for helping students overcome this obstacle?

4. Why is this a strength in student understanding?

5. Why does this strategy help leverage this strength to combat obstacles to learning?

With each question, we test the logic and the focus of the work of the I-PLC.

The final filter for innovation is the "5S concept." This basically challenges assumptions about hierarchy and traditional job expectations of employees. As it relates to teacher teams, the idea that teachers take leadership roles and question the effectiveness of other teachers' strategies is certainly foreign to the traditional structure of schools. However, the crux of the work of effective teacher teams is "collective questioning, analysis of teaching practices, deep discussion of curriculum, joint work in lesson planning, and observation and discussion of colleagues teaching" (Troen & Boles, 2012, p. 19).

Research shows that groups, regardless of the field, experience stages or periods of development on their way to becoming effective vehicles for initiating and sustaining improvements. One of the most famous portrayals of this development is the four-stage model proposed by Bruce Tuckman in 1965. Tuckman proposed that all groups go through four basic stages of development: forming, storming, norming, and performing.

In the Forming Stage, groups begin to get to know one another in relationship to the task. This occurs even when the participants are well acquainted. In addition to measuring the interpersonal dynamics, group members are trying to make meaning out of the task. This stage is often marked by an awkward niceness.

Next groups tend to move into the stage referred to as the Storming Stage. As group members learn more about one another and the task, rules of engagement may not be explicit to the point that members

Figure 6.1   Stages of Group Development

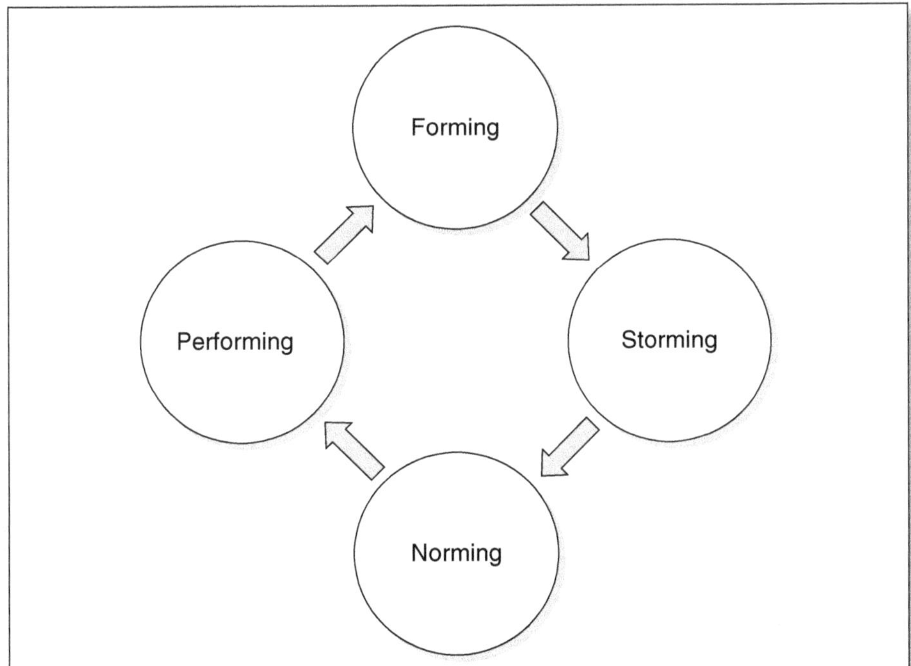

feel safe. This insecurity can lead to interpersonal conflict within the group. In this stage, the "pecking order" also begins to be established. During this stage, group members sometimes take this time to show displeasure with the task or their comfort level with group interaction by lashing out and straining internal group relations.

The next stage is called the Norming Stage. In this stage, groups begin to move the norms from being implicit to explicit. With the rules of engagement in place, members begin to feel a heightened level of safety. Similar to Abraham Maslow's (1943, 1954) Hierarchy of Needs (see Figure 6.2), the group has obtained the level of belonging and can now begin the work of focusing on the task at hand. A new level of openness also represents this stage of group dynamics.

Just as reflected in Maslow's Hierarchy of Needs, groups have to work through the levels of needs, beginning at the base by meeting the basic needs first. Then, as these base or psychological needs are met, such as food, water, and sleep, the individuals' needs move up the hierarchy to the next level. In the dynamics of a group, all individuals within the group are working through these needs on their own time. Thus, this individual battle for the meeting of these individual needs

Figure 6.2 Maslow's Hierarchy of Needs

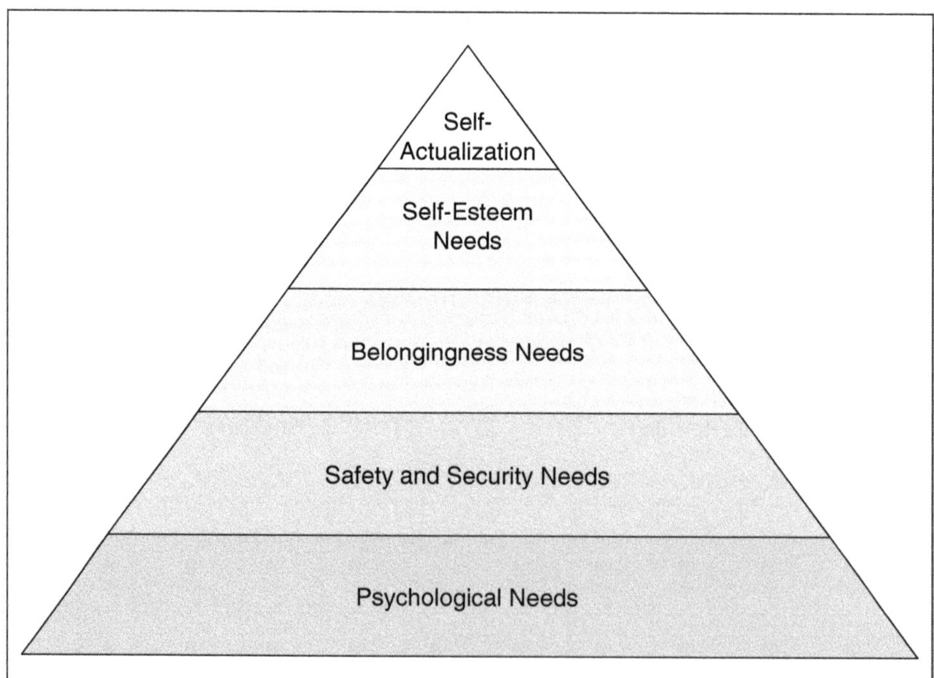

can, and often does, feed the group dynamic that manifests in the stages of group development articulated by Tuckman (Figure 6.1). Only when members of the group move into the stage where they feel that their safety needs and belongingness needs are met can the group hope to move to the norming stage and then hopefully on to where the performing stage can be realized. One of the most difficult aspects of group dynamics is that all the individuals within the group may be working through Maslow's Hierarchy of Needs simultaneously and therefore be at different levels of having their needs met. This fact can certainly have an impact on overall group dynamics at any point in time.

The final stage of group dynamics identified by Tuckman (1965) is termed the Performing Stage. Once in this stage, groups are able to work through the interpersonal needs of the individuals for the good of the group. At this point, the focus is truly on the task. In addition, collective efficacy is evident. The focus is now squarely on problem solving and task completion. As the name of the stage indicates, things begin to truly get done.

One thing to remember is that groups can continuously cycle through the four stages. Tuckman did not believe that groups simply work through one stage and then gloriously arrive at the next. More to the point, the same group can move from one stage to the next or actually skip a stage, for example from forming to norming and vice versa. This is the reason that continued support and monitoring of group behavior and dynamics is absolutely essential to the development of high-performing teams. Groups can be performing one day and storming the next. This is especially true as groups tackle new obstacles. Depending on the change of task, groups may be performing one day and move back to the stages of forming and storming the next day based on a change in task or the addition of a new member to the group. This is why we try to maintain the focus of I-PLCs on two key areas, teaching and learning, to help maintain a balance in the stages of group dynamics. This maintaining of focus also helps serve individual needs within Maslow's Hierarchy. This is why team leadership and school leadership are vital in the mission to develop and sustain effective collaboration in schools.

In preparing for the next chapter, which lays out a structured protocol for effective collaborative teaming, all these topics are key to building the solid foundation for meaningful collaboration and for consideration as school leaders and others seek to support and nurture effective collaboration within schools. The last section of this chapter summarizes why it is worthwhile.

Results of Effective Collaboration

Improved student results, period.

Effective collaboration does not just happen because we schedule time for people to sit at a table together. It takes a tremendous amount of groundwork and support. In addition, the personal benefits from engaging in the collaboration must be explicit; to evidence that through engaging in effective collaboration, teachers can improve their professional practice. As a by-product, this improved instructional ability unquestionably leads to improved student results.

Guiding Questions

1. What does collaboration currently look like in your school or system?

2. How is the impact of instructional decisions currently being evaluated in your school or district?

3. What is the topic of conversation in collaborative opportunities for teachers?

4. How do teachers receive feedback presently about their professional practice?

5. Are teachers comfortable observing other teachers and giving them feedback that is specific, honest, and actionable? Why or why not?

6. How could this process help improve teaching and learning in your school or district?

7

Impact: Professional Learning Communities

Teamwork is the secret that make common people achieve uncommon result.

Ifeanyi Enoch Onuoha

Final Vital Questions for PLCs

In the previous chapters, we dealt with the first two guiding questions for the work of professional learning communities. The first question centers on the identification of what it is that we want all students in our system to know and be able to do. We answered this question in TFM with the foundational pieces of learning intentions and the success criteria that clearly operationalize these intended learning outcomes. The second question accepts that once we have identified what is to be learned, just how do we go about determining if the knowledge and skills has been acquired or not? The answer begins with success criteria, and then goes even further with TFM foundational process of formative analysis. Finally, the last two questions pertinent to the work of PLCs is what do we do when students have gaps in their learning or understanding, and what do we do if students are already at goal or beyond? We find the answer in this chapter as we discuss the I-PLC process, which is the vehicle that drives all of the foundational work of TFM. Impact–PLCs (I-PLCs) are collaborative groups formed to search for the effect and evidence of impact of adult actions on student learning thus utilizing this knowledge and evidence to inform professional practice and improve student learning.

The Power of Professional Learning Communities

We have so many to thank for the rich literature that supports the conception of professional learning communities. The six key concepts that underlie the work of professional learning communities are the following:

1. Shared mission, vision, values and goals all focused on learning,

2. A collaborative culture with a focus on learning for all,

3. Collective inquiry into best practice and current reality,

4. Action-orientation,

5. Commitment to continuous improvement, and

6. Results-orientation. (DuFour, DuFour, & Eaker, 2008; DuFour, DuFour, Eaker, & Karhanek, 2010; Troen & Boles, 2012)

All of these key elements are embedded throughout TFM. The major difference in the Impact-Professional Learning Community is the incessant focus of the PLC on the impact that the adults are actually producing on student learning and the learning of the team. The search for impact is ongoing through the use of learning intentions, success criteria, and formative assessment. This entails studying and committing to a shared purpose of improving professional practice to ensure that we are reaching the standard set forth by John Hattie (2009, 2012) in the research of Visible Learning. The impact that we seek is a 0.40 effect size for each student for each year. This effect size Hattie found was the average effect of all 150 influences he studied in the research of Visible Learning. This metric is what Hattie termed the "hinge point." According to Hattie (2009), "The effect size of 0.40 sets a level where the effects of innovation enhance achievement in such a way that we can notice real-world differences, and this should be a benchmark of such real-world change" (p. 17). I-PLCs are interested in the effect size we are having on our students, most notably these teams question that if we are only producing an effect of less than 0.40

in a year, "why?" On the other side of the spectrum, if we are having an effect on students that measures above 0.40, we also want to ask "why" as well.

I-PLCs are also concerned with developing a common conception of what *progress* is in regard to student and adult learning. In *effective schools,* teachers understand the importance of knowing where students enter learning and how they are progressing through the journey of learning. I-PLCs use this common conception of progress and the monitoring thereof to provide the appropriate instructional support and feedback students need to be successful. Learning intentions and success criteria can aide in creating *teacher clarity* around the concept of progress (Hattie, 2012). Formative assessment should also play a role in informing teachers and students about "how they are going" and "where to next."

Professional Learning Communities that seek impact of instructional actions and interventions are in stark contrast to the many alternatives that may get caught up in other activities, such as planning school events and the like. I-PLCs are concerned with being in tune with students' levels of processing the information that is being learned to determine student progress on the learning intentions and success criteria. In addition, the depth of processing, whether surface or deep, is also important for defining progress points. The SOLO Taxonomy, which was previously introduced, is an alternative way to move beyond the focus of DOK (depth of knowledge) on alignment of standard and task, and move toward focus on seeing the progress of learning through the eyes of the student—by looking at the response provided by the student to gauge improvement. Certainly, this approach may require new learning for educators. This is why the I-PLC is just as concerned with adult learning as it is with student learning, but results are always measured in the progress of the students.

Harnessing the Power of Collaboration to Use Evidence Effectively

Much has been said about the power of collaboration, and we are finding more and more evidence to support the positive impact of structured collaboration on solving complex problems. Teachers, school leaders, and district personnel make better decisions when using the power of structured collaboration to look at things from different perspectives with differing levels of experience. Effective structured collaboration is essential for effective evidence-driven decision making. As

James Surowiecki (2005) found in the research outlined in The *Wisdom of Crowds,* groups tend to make stronger decisions than individuals. The I-PLC process is a structured collaborative method that harnesses the power of individuals through a structured protocol that helps educators at the district level, the school level, and the classroom level make better, more informed decisions.

Stephen White (2011) stated in his book *Beyond the Numbers,* "Collaboration is essential in data analysis if we are to get beyond the numbers" (p. 55). This is to say that if we are truly going to go deeper than identifying simple patterns in data to actually determining root causes, then we must use the power of collaboration to provide the diversity needed to filter the data from multiple points of view. A great deal of research has been done over the past 20 years surrounding effective collaboration within schools (Berry, Daughtrey, & Wieder, 2009; Carol, Fulton, & Doerr, 2010; DuFour et al., 2008; Hattie, 2009, 2012; White, 2011). All the research points to the fact that there is great power to solve many of the complex problems when educators come together in a structured collaborative process with a focus on teaching and learning. A research study titled *Team up for 21st Century Teaching and Learning: What Research and Practice Reveal about Professional Learning,* which was conducted by the National Commission on Teaching and America's Future (Carol et al., 2010) condensed much of the research around effective structured collaboration into a set of principles required for successful collaboration. Similar to these findings, the following six principles underpin the work of the I-PLC process within TFM.

- Principle 1—**Shared Values and Goals**—All actions of the learning teams should focus on student learning and or seeking evidence of the impact of teacher and leadership actions on student results. This concept of constantly seeking the evidence of adult impact should drive the mission of the team and the goals that are set.
- Principle 2—**Collective Responsibility**—It is critical that all members of the learning team are committed to the success of all students. When measuring the impact of adult actions, it is not enough to measure the mean or the average impact across all students, the team has the moral responsibility to identify the impact of adult actions on each individual student. All means all.
- Principle 3—**Authentic Assessment**—The commitment to the formative analysis process revolves around the use of assessment to inform teaching and learning on the part of the teachers,

the leaders, and the students. Authenticity is derived from assessments that are used to elicit real-time evidence about how students are performing in relation to the learning intentions as measured by clearly articulated success criteria that are clearly understood by the students. Students are explicitly taught assessment practices and how to use the evidence to determine next steps.

- Principle 4—**Self-Directed Reflection**—The ending and the beginning of each I-PLC cycle begins with setting goals and ends with the reevaluation of the goals in relation to predetermined success criteria. Inherently, TFM is a process that aligns long-, mid-, and short-term goals and sets about connecting adult strategies to identified student needs in relationship to the impact of these adult actions on student achievement of the goals.

- Principle 5—**Stable Settings**—The I-PLC meetings are a structured protocol for teachers to effectively talk to other teachers about the impact of their teaching on learners. Teacher leadership is critical within the process as well as a collective commitment to take a problem-solving approach to the obstacles to student learning. Meetings are not about personalities but about the evidence of the impact of the teams teaching on the learning.

- Principle 6—**Strong Leadership Support**—There is not a single process that is worthwhile to effective schooling that can take place without effective leadership. TFM makes the role of instructional leadership manageable at the system and school levels. School leaders may not be expert in every content area, but they can be expert in effective inquiry, the seeking of evidence of the impact of strategies or interventions, and the effective use of formative assessment data to make real-time decisions in relation to teaching and learning. (Based on Carol, Fulton, & Doerr, 2010, pp. 9–10)

Impact-PLCs—Shared Mission, Vision, Values, and Goals

Impact PLCs have the mind-set that all students and educators have the ability to reach high standards of performance with the proper amount of support and feedback. A common unifying concept of I-PLCs at all levels within the system is what Carol Dweck (2006) calls a "Growth Mindset." An individual, or team, with a growth mind-set believes that ability can be improved by deliberate practice and supportive guidance. Natural ability is simply a starting point, not a self-fulfilling prophecy.

This mind-set is essential as the team works together to solve the most complex issues affecting teaching, learning, and leadership. Hattie found that the consequences of expectations of teachers in the classroom have a very large effect ($d = .43$) on student success. Looking back to our previous discussion of Hattie's (2012) work with *Visible Learning,* this effect is well over the "hinge-point" of $d = .40$ that Hattie found to be roughly equivalent to one solid year of growth in student achievement (p. 3). It is possible to then multiply these effects as we consider the expectations at the school and district level as well. The classroom is on the frontline of setting expectations for beliefs in students and teachers, but we cannot discount the impact of expectations at the school and system levels. If we hope to expand the islands of excellence often found in solitary schools across districts, developing a common language of professional practice is vital. In addition, to sustain improvement it is critical that successful innovations are supported and promoted at the district level.

I-PLCs—Collective Responsibility

Collaboration comes from the Latin *collaborates* which means to "labor together" (Merriam-Webster, 2013a). Part of the gel that holds the collective group together is a collective sense of accountability for the success of all students and educators. As Stephen White (2011) correctly states, "Data of any kind are only meaningful when professionals collaboratively examine, analyze, reflect, and ultimately decide to act on data available to them" (p. 55). This decision to act implies a commitment to being responsible for the results. According to Peter Senge (2000), "At its core, team learning is a discipline of practices designed, over time, to get the people of a team thinking and acting together. The team members need not think alike" (p. 70). Therefore, even though the team works together to a collective end, all still maintain individual responsibility to work toward the common goal.

The initial meeting of any I-PLC focuses on the setting of norms for how the work and meetings are conducted. As the team works through its initial development, it is vitally important that all play a role in the development of what become the rules for engagement.

Making it a collective responsibility to focus on the following general norms is vital to the success of the learning team:

1. All team members commit to maintain the focus of the team meeting on learning for both adults and students.

2. All team members commit to contributing to the success of the team by following through with action.

3. All team members commit to follow through on the decisions reached by the team, but also agree that discussing divergent solutions is important to ensuring the final decision is made even stronger.

4. The team maintains a growth mind-set.

5. Decisions are based on evidence, both positive and negative, from quality sources and focus on improving student and adult learning.

This is just a simple sample of some of the cursory obligations that team members must be willing to make to demonstrate a mutual commitment to the work of the team. This collective responsibility and promise is essential if the team is to function effectively.

I-PLCs—Authentic Assessments

The types of assessment tools used by I-PLCs are the formative assessments described in Chapter 5, "Formative Analysis." These assessments are generated by groups of teachers to provide the teachers with information about student knowledge and ability in relation to essential learning intentions. Teachers using this process effectively, see themselves as "students of their own teaching" (Hattie, 2012, p. 14) by looking for the success or lack thereof in the instructional strategies chosen that lead to the effects seen in student results. The most important aspect here is that the focus is on the strategy and the results, not personality or teaching style. I-PLCs make decisions based on evidence of impact because the team is founded on the undeniable research that in schools teachers have the most significant impact on student achievement, and school leadership has the second most significant impact (Leithwood, Seashore Louis, Anderson, & Wahlstrom, 2010).

In a national study titled *Collaboration: Closing the Effective Teaching Gap* (Berry et al., 2009) that included more than 1,200 teachers, The Center for Teacher Quality (CTQ) found that structured teacher collaboration could be critical in ensuring higher teacher quality from classroom to classroom. There were some best practices surrounding effective collaboration identified in the CTQ study; the recommendations of best practice for collaboration were the following:

1. Scheduling adequate time for collaboration.

2. Aligning collaboration structures for both horizontal and vertical collaboration.

3. Structuring formal collaboration meetings.

4. Creating an atmosphere of mutual trust. (Berry et al., 2009, pp. 6–7)

Looking back on the findings of the study by the National Commission on Teaching and America's Future, some common themes emerge, specifically in the recommendations that collaboration needs to be structured and that it definitively must be scheduled. The I-PLC process certainly provides a structured impact-driven decision-making protocol that follows the recommendations of best practice for effective collaboration at the system, school, and classroom levels. This shows a commitment that the evidence of the impact of the collaboration will be measured by student results. Most notably, these results will revolve around improvements in student success within the context of the intentional implementation of targeted instructional and leadership strategies.

In the end, whether looking at leadership or instructional strategies, success will ultimately be measured by direct evidence of positive impact on student results. Finally, when leadership makes the commitment to supporting effective structured collaboration, then leadership will certainly make it a priority that these meetings are scheduled and championed. The role of assessment in the I-PLC process then is to provide real-time evidence of the impact of the system, school, or classroom on student learning from evidence obtained through authentic assessments in the formative analysis process.

I-PLCs—Self-Directed Reflection

I-PLCs use the learning intentions and success criteria as their foundation. From these two essential elements, teachers develop formative assessment tools to use as a pre-assessment for the students even before the team starts any instruction on the learning intentions and success criteria. Once the team members have the results from the formative assessment, they bring the evidence back to the I-PLC meeting. Here the learning team goes through the protocol of the I-PLC process whereby they drill down into data and set goals, analyze student results, and hypothesize theories of action that the team can use to directly target student learning needs. From here, teams finally determine checkpoint assessment tasks that they will use in an ongoing manner to monitor the impact of the hypothesized strategies. Using the learning intentions, success criteria, and assessment evidence to formulate theories of action, I-PLCs can expect to see student behaviors indicative of improved student results related to the effective implementation of the strategy—if the appropriate strategy has been chosen. Therefore, the entire instructional process becomes a search for evidence of impact and success, or a lack thereof. In turn, this evidence then is used to provide feedback to teachers and students alike about the progress both are making in the classroom in regard to teaching and learning, neither one being mutually exclusive. John Hattie (2009) found in the research surrounding Visible Learning:

> What is most important is that teaching is visible to the student and that the learning is visible to the teacher. The more the student becomes the teacher and the more the teacher becomes the learner, then the more successful the outcomes. (p. 25)

Hattie in no way advocates that teachers are simply to be the "guide on the side" and become passive in the instructional process. On the contrary, Hattie (2009) explains, "visible teaching relates to teachers as activators, as deliberate change agents, and as directors of learning" (p. 25). On the opposite end of the spectrum, this does not advocate teachers standing before students and doing what Hattie calls "drilling and trilling to the less than willing" (p. 25). It does involve teachers seeking the impact of their teaching in the results they are seeing in the students. By using the data from measuring and evaluating strategies that have an impact on students' learning, teachers can make real-time decisions and inferences about which strategies are or are not working. At the same time, teachers work within the collaborative groups to explore more deeply the possible root causes of student misconceptions and strategies for attacking errors in student understanding. This also involves self-reflection for teachers as they make determinations about what went well and what did not, and most important, why or why not? This type of evidence-based inquiry and reflection is at the core of the I-PLC process.

I-PLCs—Stable Settings

I-PLCs maintain the focus on teaching and learning. Whether organized into vertical teams, for example, Grades 3, 4, and 5 language arts teachers, or horizontally, such as a ninth-grade transition center team featuring Grade 9 language arts, Grade 9 math, Grade 9 science, and so on, these teams maintain a focus on learning for the teachers and the students they serve. Discussions are grounded in the evidence provided by formative assessments that provide the basis for the formative analysis process where students' strengths and weakness are clarified in relation to the learning intentions and success criteria. The conversations must focus on strategies and the impact of those strategies on students' real-time prioritized needs. The goal is for teachers to be able to provide instruction and feedback at the appropriate "plus 1" level required to foster student academic growth.

As part of the team formation, group norms are developed to help maintain this focus and clearly articulate the ground rules for the interactions within the team. Most of all, these rules should establish a climate of trust so that all can share in the powerful work of collaborative problem solving. The power of collaboration rests in the ability to look at problems from different perspectives and different experiences. To get the most of the process, teams must foster the climate of safety so that all members feel supported by their colleagues on the team. I-PLCs are not about Teacher A's students, Teacher B's students, Teacher C's students, and so on, but the team takes on the responsibility that these students are all *OUR* students! As a team, each member takes ownership of the students, the decisions made, and the results. Each member of the team is treated with the respect and the admiration of a highly capable professional educator. The tricky thing is that in order for respect to be maintained, it must be earned. This means that each member of the I-PLC takes on not only the collective responsibility of the results of the team, but also the individual responsibility for contributing to the success of the team. The adage rings true when it comes to teams:

T — *together*
E — *each*
A — *achieves*
M — *more*

I-PLCs—Strong Leadership Support

One of the most important aspects in implementing effective I-PLCs is the support and direction provided by the leadership at the system, school, and classroom levels. Leadership is critical in helping all organizations maintain focus, monitor results, and continue in the belief that the work the organization is doing will lead to meaningful results. These are leadership responsibilities that must be attended to at all levels within districts if the goal is sustainable school improvement.

At the system level, there must be a commitment to proper training, and the time needed to support the deep implementation of the I-PLC process. The process is the pinnacle of the larger focus model. For it to function at maximum effectiveness, time should be taken to deeply execute the foundational pieces of identifying the learning intentions and success criteria. These learning progressions derived from the academic content standards are the guideposts that teams use to ensure success for all students. I-PLC discussions center around seeking to ensure that all students have the knowledge, skills, and dispositions needed to be successful on these learning intentions and success criteria that have been deemed critical for success in college and careers, and which can certainly determine student opportunities after school.

Next, the I-PLC develops a scope and sequence or inquiry calendar to ensure appropriate exposure to the learning intentions and success criteria within units of study as the year unfolds. Once the units of study (usually lasting anywhere from two to four weeks), are populated with the learning intentions and success criteria, then teachers, students, and parents have a much clearer picture of what students need to know and be able to do to be considered proficient on the grade-level academic content standards for the year. After the process for creating the learning intentions and success criteria is complete, I-PLCs begin planning the periodic formative assessment tasks and formative pre- and post-assessments used to measure student understanding and provide the real-time feedback that drives the formative analysis process.

As soon as the results are analyzed at the individual classroom level, teachers are now ready to utilize the I-PLC process to look at all students in that particular course, grade level, or content area depending on how the team is structured. This is the beauty of the I-PLC process. Any group of educators, even interdisciplinary teachers can collaborate using this structure just as long as they are joined together by common learning intentions and success criteria, or common problems of practice or learning.

The interconnectedness of the various foundational pieces is crucial for successful implementation. This focus and commitment are more easily generated when individual school sites can be assured that they have the full support of the district in the implementation of TFM. This is not to say that an individual school cannot have success implementing this model on their own if they have the resources to do so, but normally the professional learning calendar and funding is most easily aligned to support this work when support is obtained at the system level.

School-level leadership is also irreplaceable when implementing a model for improvement as far reaching and comprehensive as TFM. Ultimately, it falls to the school-level leadership to help PLCs maintain focus, oversee effective implementation of the I-PLC protocol, and monitor the results of effective use of the I-PLC process to improve student achievement. Last, school-level leaders are charged with maintaining the growth mind-set that is needed as a foundation for successful PLC's seeking to ensure success for all students and all teachers on the learning intentions and success criteria.

The most essential level of leadership for the I-PLC process is at the classroom level. PLC leaders are vital in ensuring that teams remain focused on the teaching and learning. These leaders are not expected to take on the administrative duties of evaluation or discipline in the case of team members who are not living up to the established norms of the team. Team leaders are expected to help maintain the focus of the teams' work on the evidence of impact and serve as leaders in helping to build and maintain the efficacy of team members in the process. Team leaders must have a growth mind-set and believe in the potential of all students and all teachers. This leadership role is so critical to the success of the I-PLC process that school leaders should meet with PLC leaders periodically, a minimum of at least once per month, to seek ways that the school-level leadership can continually improve and support the work of the I-PLC. This allows time for PLC leaders to share successes and hindrances to the teams meeting their ultimate goal of success for all students and teachers.

In the end, TFM is driven by the great work of teachers talking to teachers about teaching and learning and then taking decisive action based on evidence. This requires effective leadership support at the classroom, school, and system levels to ensure success for all.

I-PLCs at the System Level

Ultimately, the I-PLC process is about inquiry. At the system level, this process fits very well with the concerns of a high functioning system leadership team with a focus on improving the teaching and learning within the district, that is, that our schools are effectually using evidence to determine the relative impact of our instructional and leadership strategies in real time across all grade levels and then taking decisive action based on this evidence. This team should consist of the superintendent, directors, members of the school board, community leaders, parents, and even students. The idea is that we have a structured way of looking at the results that we receive with our students and evaluate the impact that these strategies (enacted by the adults in the system) have on our students. Once we gather this evidence of impact, this then sets the foundation for the formulation of action theories that become strategies to be used in response to continuous improvement.

From a strategy perspective, a major point to monitor in the context of a system-level PLC is to determine the depth of implementation at the school level at all sites within the school system. System-level personnel can be attuned to monitoring and gathering evidence of implementation at the various school sites across the district. Therefore, if 40 percent of the classroom PLCs are functioning at a mastery level, then we can articulate that by saying that the building has roughly 40 percent implementation of the I-PLC process. This data is then correlated to student results on formative assessments and other district benchmark measures that are aligned to the learning intentions and success criteria. System PLCs can support the efforts of the school-level PLCs by providing the support and training necessary to ensure deeper implementation. Doug Reeves (2010b) found in his research for the book *Transforming Professional Development into Student Results* that only by getting to higher levels of implementation can districts or schools hope to reflect high impact in student results. This means that just having 50 percent to 60 percent implementation does not cut it. To be systematic, implementation needs to be at the 90 percent level or above. Only then can we expect to see the full impact of the power of effective structured collaboration, the tight alignment of instruction and assessment to the learning intentions and success criteria, and the effective use of formative assessment and feedback. This type of feedback requires that superintendents and directors spend a great deal of time within the schools themselves collecting observational evidence. This type of support goes along with a commitment to making the types of systematic changes needed for schools to make efficient improvements in teaching and learning.

One strategy for making this a reality is to schedule periodic meetings with the school-level I-PLCs to discuss level of implementation, progress, and provide the teams the time to present their goals and status to the system-level I-PLC. Rudy Giuliani credits using similar types of meetings with the department heads for the city of New York in helping his mayoral administration to turn around some of the city's most troublesome problems, such as crime, government inefficiency, and lack of overall safety. Giuliani (2002, p. 72) called this innovative approach to tackling serious problems at a system level, "Compstat," which stands for Comparative Statistics. This process was so successful that in 1996, the Compstat program won the Innovations in Government Award from Harvard. In these meetings, members of various agencies were asked to perform five basic functions in a presentation before the system-level management: (1) utilize data to make an honest assessment of current status, (2) identify and clarify goals, (3) draw attention to strategies that have led to positive outcomes, (4) acknowledge trouble spots and possible next steps, and (5) brainstorm next steps for the toughest dilemmas. In a school system setting, meetings of this nature can certainly be shaped around the concept of the I-PLC, where school-level teams would be asked to perform a similar five functions around the single idea of what impact we are having on student results and the strategies we are currently using to achieve these results.

I-PLCs at the School Level

School-level PLCs are concerned with the level of functioning of the various classroom-level PLCs on site. Once again, we can create a clear set of expectations for the proficient implementation of the I-PLC process, school-level PLCs can monitor effective implementation of the I-PLC process at the classroom level. In addition, school-level I-PLCs will also look to student results on formative assessments used by the classroom I-PLCs in the formative analysis process. Documentation of the meetings containing the evidence that teachers within the teams are using to make the decisions that lead to the selection of instructional strategies and the creation of theories of action can also be used for evaluation of the effective implementation of these meetings. School I-PLC members can circulate into and out of the classroom I-PLC meetings, additionally, school-level I-PLC members can also get a good picture of the implementation and the impact on student results by using the documentation (e.g., next-steps and minutes recording important decision points arrived at during the meeting) provided after each classroom I-PLC meeting. Also, in Step 6 of the seven-step I-PLC process is where teams articulate "If–Then" statements. These "If–Then" statements, or theories of action, are pictures of what the proactive strategies will look like if implemented with fidelity and also describe what behaviors and products we can expect to see from students if the selected strategies are having the intended successful impact. "If–Then" statements make excellent "look-fors" for classroom walk-though observations where school leaders and/or peers might give specific feedback to colleagues about the implementation of the selected strategies. This gives the teacher another set of eyes, as it were, within the classroom to provide the teacher feedback about the level of implementation of the approved strategy. Many teachers appreciate this feedback from peers, especially if they are implementing a new strategy. Ideally, they had time to practice this strategy with peers and receive some feedback before trying it in the classroom for the first time in the context of the I-PLC meeting. This lesson study is an important part of the I-PLC process. We discuss the use of formative assessment evidence and analysis in great detail in this book, but this does not mean that I-PLCs are not also involved in the more traditional work of PLCs, such as collaborative analyzing of student work, practicing new instructional strategies and techniques, and collaborative planning. These are all valuable functions of the I-PLC at the classroom level, but the vast majority of the work is seeking the impact of instruction by looking at the teaching through the eyes of students and the evidence of learning present in formative assessment tasks.

I-PLCs at the Classroom Level

When looking at the factors attributable to schools, teachers have the highest impact on school achievement. We have used the cliché for years in education that "what teachers do matters" (Hattie, 2012, p. 15). From the research in *Visible Learning*, John Hattie (2012) found that the reality is really, "what certain teachers do matters" (pp. 15–16). According to Hattie's *Visible Learning* (2009, 2012) research, the teacher is the greatest source of variance in achievement results within schools. This being the case, teachers are now seeing the value of working together with colleagues to solve the complex issues involved with helping all students reach high levels of learning.

In the CTQ study (Berry et al., 2009), which surveyed more than 1,200 teachers across the nation, researchers found that nearly 60 percent of teachers engaged in collaborative groups did so with the hope of being able to share ideas and effective strategies. In addition, when teachers were asked where they receive help and guidance on issues related to teaching, 68 percent said they specifically look to other teachers for answers. Teachers who were involved in effective structured collaborative groups reported that they felt much more support in their classroom practice than those teachers who were not engaged in effective collaborative teams. Last, studies show that students perform better on tests of reading and mathematics (Goddard & Goddard, 2007) when their teachers are involved in effective learning teams that provide structure for "teachers to talk to each other about teaching" (Hattie, 2012, p. 60).

I-PLCs at the classroom level are where the "rubber meets the road" when it comes to effective problem solving and deciding on issues of teaching and learning. I-PLCs are teams of teachers engaged in selecting specific strategies to address student needs identified using real-time assessments. Instructional impact is measured by looking to student results for determining better solutions attained by drawing on the expertise of the group. The process is about using assessment elicited evidence to arrive at valid inferences through formative analysis and then using these inferences to select the best strategies to meet student needs. It is a teacher-driven process aimed at ensuring better results for students, teachers, schools, and districts.

Adult Action and Student Results

The mind-set that underpins the I-PLC process is based on the overwhelming research that the actions of the adults in schools can have an impact equal to and even above factors outside the school. Hattie found influence after influence within the direct control of the school, teacher, and leadership that had effect sizes on student achievement much larger than some of the outside influences that students bring to school. For example, the influences of "Home Environment" and "Socioeconomic Status" had a significant effect size on student achievement ($d = .52$; Hattie, 2012, p. 252). Nevertheless, Hattie (2009, 2012) found numerous influences attributed as contributions from teachers to student achievement with significantly higher effects, such as "Teacher Credibility ($d = 0.90$)" (Hattie, 2012, p. 267), "Providing Formative Evaluation ($d = .90$)" (Hattie, 2012, p. 181), and "Piagetian Programs ($d = 1.28$)" (p. 43). In many cases, teacher influences had the capacity to contribute twice the effect of either the home environment category or socioeconomic status.

Figure 7.1 demonstrates the importance of the mission of the I-PLC to monitor impact by looking at the implementation of a high likelihood strategy (for example, I-PLCs) with all the intended benefits of increasing the effect size related to student results over the course of a year. This figure illustrates the fact that if the strategy chosen is implemented with fidelity, then we should see some impact on student achievement results over a year, which is represented in the following example as effect size.

Because we know from a preponderance of the research (Hattie, 2009, 2012; Leithwood, Seashore Louis, Anderson, & Wahlstrom, 2004; Leithwood et al., 2010; Marzano 2003, 2007; Reeves, 2006, 2011) that instructional and leadership strategies employed by the adults in the building have significant effect on student achievement, then we also know that when we isolate these strategies as variables applied to instruction and leadership behaviors by adults, we can assume there should be some relationship between the impact of these strategies on student results and the level at which these strategies are implemented. The key is that if a strategy is worthwhile, we should see some impact of the use of that strategy in student results. Ideally, as the strategy is implemented more effectively, as represented by the positive side of the x-axis in Figure 7.1, student results start to increase, in this example measured by effect size. This in no way assumes that correlation is equal to causation. Anytime we implement a "high-likelihood" strategy supported by research the recognition is that if implemented properly, it has a "high-likelihood" of producing improved results. Nevertheless, we know that

Figure 7.1 Illustrative Example of I-PLC Implementation vs. Effect Size on Student

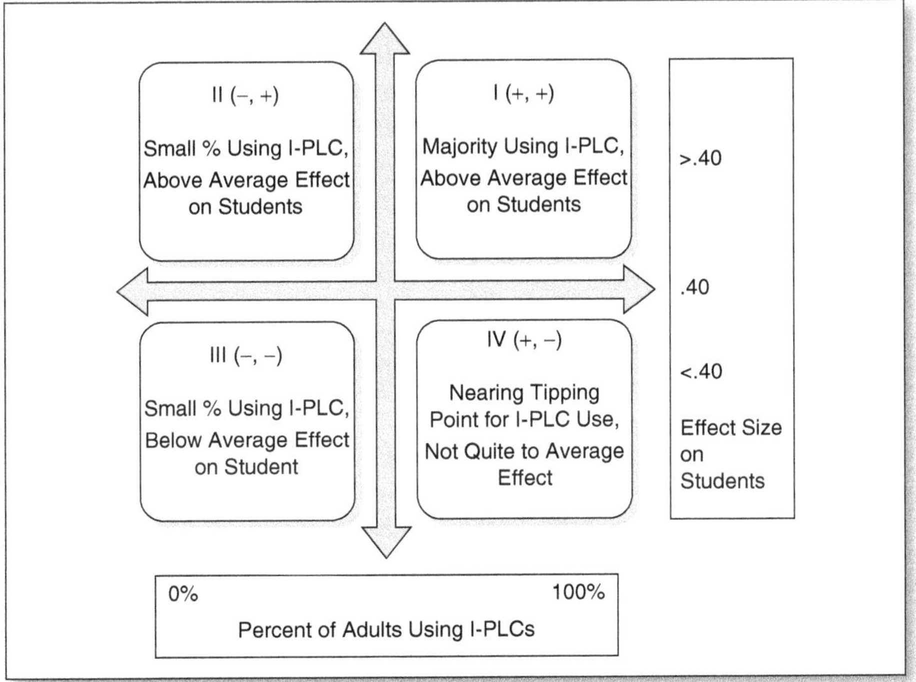

there is no 100 percent guarantee that just by implementing this strategy we are assured of improved results. This is one more reason why the ongoing process of formative analysis conducted through the I-PLC is so important. The I-PLC requires a constant search for evidence of impact in regard to adult actions and student results; it does not assume anything.

Effective evidence-based decision making requires that we look at both the adults' actions and the students' results if we truly are going to harness the power of data to make real-time improvements to instruction and learning. Research is clear to the point that if we want higher student results, then we have to recognize the power of our behaviors (strategies), continuously seek evidence of the impact of those strategies, and use this evidence of that impact to provide accurate, specific, and timely feedback to the entire system.

Important Questions to Guide Inquiry

Because schools suffer from an oversupply of data, it is vitally important that educators clearly define what evidence they seek about student learning and the strategies employed to produce this learning. This focused inquiry begins with educators formulating guiding questions about the system and student learning. Some examples are as follows:

Example 1

Would an increase in the frequency (number of minutes, times per week, etc.) of direct instruction by Grade 5 math teachers in the specific concept of number sense, help increase student proficiency for ELL male students in two-step arithmetic problems on the district benchmark assessments *(assumes these assessments are aligned to high-stakes state assessment)*?

Example 2

Would an increase in the number of minutes students spend in writing workshops with Grade 7 language arts teachers increase student proficiency in organizing nonfiction argumentative writing organization for all students on the district benchmarks assessments *(assumes these assessments are aligned to high-stakes state assessment)*?

These questions guide the search for evidence to determine strategies aimed at addressing the specific deficits that students exhibit on successive years of data, if available, or in real time if using the

I-PLC process within a current instructional cycle. It is not so much that these questions facilitate the gathering of more data. In actuality, these questions guide inquiry. It is the collection of information and evidence about the relationship of the use of specific strategies to specific changes or improvements in student learning that is the goal for evidence-based decision making. As stated by Booth, Colomb, and Williams (2003), "new knowledge depends on the questions you ask—and don't" (p. 4) of those involved in the inquiry process. In addition, the idea is to generate questions that everyone in the school feels compelled and vested in finding the answers. When developing these effective research questions, professional educators can follow this pattern adapted from recommendations in Booth et al. (2003, pp. 46–47):

1. Identify the important learning issues and how they relate. Use Systems Thinking for this determination.

2. Trace the history of possible learning issues within the data, and how these findings might play a role in the history of school achievement.

3. Identify the characteristics and the categories of learning (factual, conceptual, procedural, metacognitive) of the learning issues and that these issues might include.

4. Determine the impact that discovering the answer to these questions could have on the overall performance of the school.

Searching the Evidence

To determine the focus of the important questions that guide inquiry, it is vital that educators dig deeply into the numbers to get as close to the root cause for deficits in learning as possible so that the strategies chosen are aimed at altering errors in thinking and performing. This process of going deeper into the data can be done by using a set of simple questions to narrow the focus. The following are examples of questions for discovery of the data that can be used to narrow the inquiry:

Evidence Focus Questions for the Student Data

1. What subject area is in need of the most improvement?

2. Which specific group (ethnicity, gender, socioeconomic status, language proficiency, etc.) of students is most in need of improvement?

3. Where does this specific group of students need the most support, within the broader subject area of Question 1?

4. What identifiable knowledge, skills, and dispositions does this specific group of students need to improve performance in this selected area?

Action Focus Questions for the Adult Actions

1. What improvement is needed the most in our specific subject area?

2. What specific group (ethnicity, gender, socioeconomic status, language proficiency, etc.) of students is in most in need of improvement?

3. What inferences can we make, based on formative evidence, about the root causes of the learning obstacles for this group of students? What inferences can we make, based on formative evidence, about their strengths?

4. What theories of action can we create that directly targets the prioritized needs of students?

I-PLC Foundation

The foundation of the I-PLC process is threefold. The first key foundational pieces are the development of the learning intentions from the broader academic content standards. Classroom PLCs use these learning intentions as the basis for the building of formative assessments to gather evidence, and ultimately, move to the formative analysis process, which is an ongoing look at multiple sources of formative data. School-level I-PLCs monitor the success of students on these learning intentions by the formative analysis process and tracking the effective implementation of each process step of the various I-PLCs within the school. System-level I-PLCs support the implementation of the learning intentions via the evaluation of student results on formative assessments and district benchmark assessments throughout the school term. Support at the school and system level is crucial for the function and sustainability of I-PLCs at the classroom level.

Once the learning intentions are identified, the second foundational practice is defining the success criteria. That is the process where teachers make clear the learning intentions contained within the standards by intentionally identifying the knowledge, skills, and dispositions required of students to show mastery of the broader overall standards. Remember from earlier discussions that classroom-, school-, and system-level I-PLCs examine the degree to which all tasks and assessments are aligned to the learning intentions and success criteria.

The third and final foundational piece supporting the I-PLC process is that of formative analysis. Involving much more than teachers giving a formative test, formative analysis begins with the building, administration, and scoring of a formative assessment. After that step, the true work begins when teacher teams (either arranged by grade level, comparable course, or common problem of practice), work together to make inferences about student understanding and ability based on impact evidence from the assessment. This formative analysis is embedded within TFM's process (see Figure 7.2).

Figure 7.2   The Focus Model

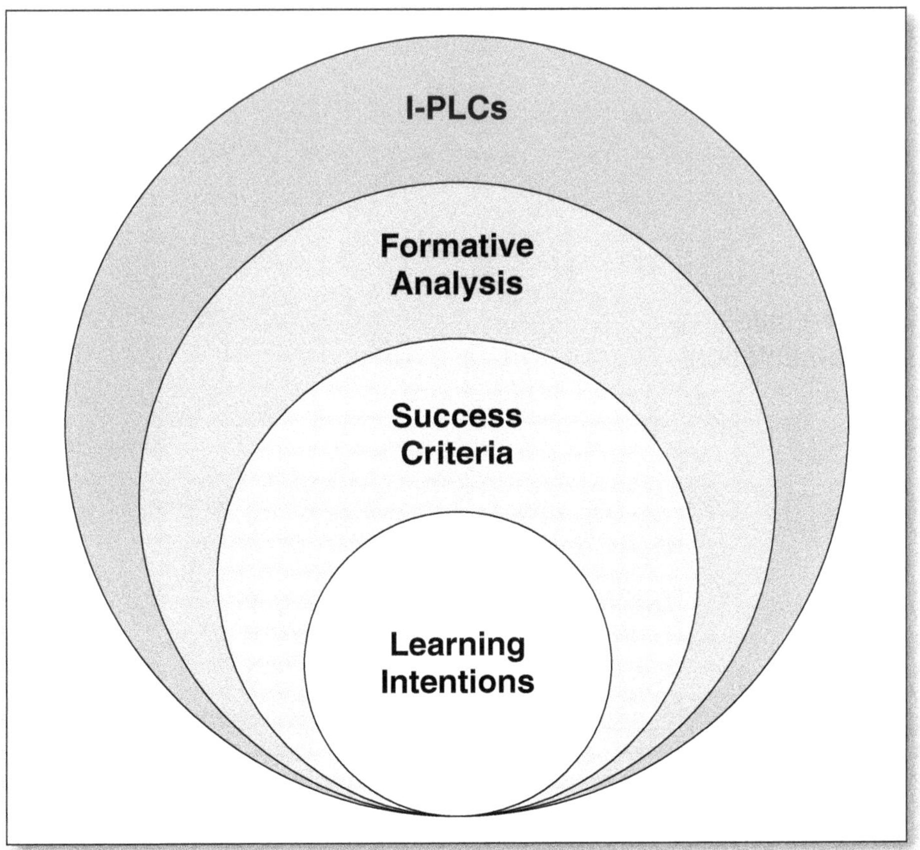

The seven steps of the I-PLC process spell **S²MARTER**. The hope is that by following the seven step decision making model of the I-PLC method, both teachers and students will make more informed (smarter) decisions about teaching and learning. The descriptions of the seven steps are seen in Figure 7.3.

Step 1: Search the Data and Set Goals

Step 1 begins the process of evidence-based decision making by looking at archival data that might generate questions or concerns about

Figure 7.3   7-Step I-PLC Process

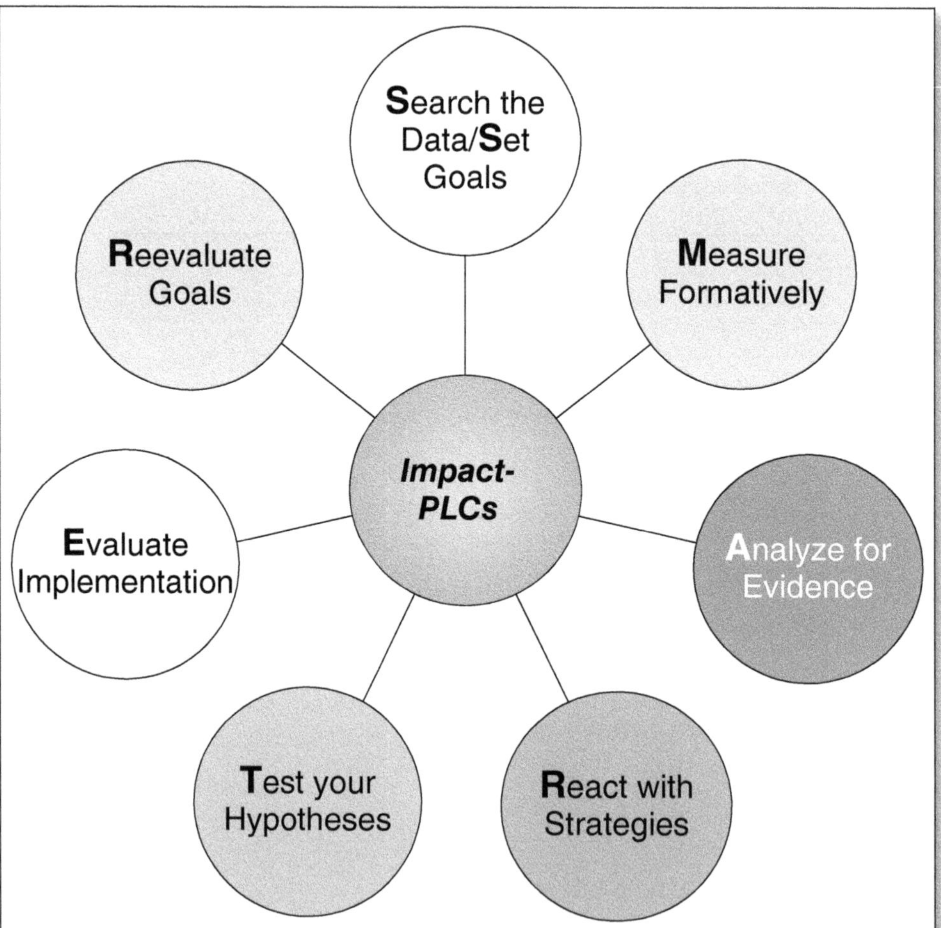

Adapted from the Iowa Professional Development Model Framework (2009); Irwin and Farr (2004); Birenbaum, Kimron, Shilton, and Shahaf-Barzilay (2010); and *Professional Learning Plans* by Killion and Learning Forward (2013).

student performance and learning. Ideally, we gather 3 years of data or more for this analysis. The intent is to make an evidence-supported inference about the area of greatest need or most pressing issues regarding student learning to direct the focus of our long-term and midterm goals. In so doing, we narrow the focus of the collaborative structure at the microlevel of the classroom I-PLC. This analysis should occur at the beginning of the school improvement plan development process. As the evidence is analyzed, not only are we looking for areas of "low performance," but we are also looking for those areas where performance is "high." The goal is to identify those areas we can focus on for improvement, and to accentuate the positive performance in order to see if this success can be replicated in other areas of the school. Once these areas are identified, teams set both long-term goals (2 to 5 years) and midterm SMARTER goals of 6 to 12 months. Notice the addition of the *ER* to the common acronym "SMART" in reference to goals. This concept is attributed to Sir Michael Barber, a leading authority on education systems and education reform. The *E* simply adds the idea that we need to evaluate the goal continuously. The *Merriam-Webster* (2014) dictionary defines *evaluate* as "to judge the value or condition of (*someone or something*) in a careful and thoughtful way." In regard to the work of the I-PLC, we are constantly seeking the magnitude of the learning (*the something*) and the measurable impact of the teacher and student (*the someone*). The *R* references that because of the formative nature of the actions we employ in pursuit of our goals, and as we are testing the hypotheses of new adjustments, or strategies, it is incumbent for us to reevaluate our goals in light of any new evidence, positive or negative, that might present itself as a representation of the teachers' or students' impact. These are the end goals that the micro activity of the classroom-level I-PLC sets in motion as they work on the shorter-term (from two to six weeks) SMARTER goals related to each instructional cycle supporting implementation of specific learning intentions. Ultimately, the short-term goals of the I-PLC cycles should be directly aligned to the long-term and midterm goals of the school-level I-PLC. Finally, if coherence is evident within the system, there should also be some semblance of alignment with the broader school-improvement goals at the district level as well.

All these school goals, long, mid, and short term, are also necessarily aligned to the long-term goals found at the system level or state level improvement plan that normally spans 3 years or more. It is at this stage where TFM separates itself from other school improvement plans; other plans talk about the need to align goals and actions, but the reality is that only TFM is designed to do so from the outset.

The resulting outcome of Step one to search the data and set goals is a clear understanding of what the broad focus will be for the year as we move into the in-depth process of addressing our most pressing needs as articulated by the long-term and midterm goals for the I-PLC. All action by the team focuses on reaching the improvement articulated in the goal. Example goals from this step might look like the following:

Step 1 Midterm Goal—Math for a Middle School I-PLC

By May 4, we will improve math achievement in the coming year in Grade 6 math from 40 percent (40/100) of students scoring proficient and above on the Grade 6 end-of-year (EOY) assessment to 68.7 percent (69/100) proficient and above in order to reach the required adequate yearly progress (AYP) requirements of students proficient and above.

Set SMARTER Goals

Viviane Robinson (2011) speaks of the importance of goals in learning because the goal itself points out the discrepancy between where we are to where we want to go. John Hattie (2009, 2012) also found that goal setting that results in action has a significant effect size (effect size $d = .50$, where effect size $d = .40$ is equivalent to one year of academic gain in student achievement). Within the I-PLC process, goal setting is a vital part of Step 1 as we seek to improve the achievement level of all performance groups in the long term, the midterm, and the short term. The point that TFM leads with the setting of goals makes the process unique from other collaborative protocols.

Using the acronym SMARTER, the "S" stands for *specificity* in that we are working toward mastery of specific learning intentions. The "M" provides a quantifiable *metric* that we seek to increase from the initial formative evaluation provided to the student to the post-assessment that follows instruction using the strategies paired to students' most urgent needs within the identified performance groups. Using the research of John Hattie (2012) as a base, it is recommended that the "A" stand for the setting of an *ambitious goal*. Hattie found that only when goals are set that stretch students at the "+1 level" (2012, p. 113) do we truly set the challenge high enough to cause growth in learning. This plays out in schools across the nation because the schools have multiple students who may come into the instructional unit more than one grade level below expectations. Simply setting a goal for one year's academic growth with this group does not begin to get students moving toward the grade-level performance needed for them to be considered proficient on grade-level standards. In this case, we need to set challenging goals and expectations for these students and then support them in working toward these ambitious goals. When setting SMARTER goals, we certainly want them to be relevant, thus the "R," which stands for relevancy of the *learning intention(s),* which is the subject of focus in our classroom-level I-PLC cycle. Finally, the "T" stands for team to stress that all members of the team need to stay on the same page and timetable: specifically, about when they assess, when they relay that data to the team, when they engage in formative assessment tasks throughout the unit, and when they produce post-assessments and communicate that evidence to the I-PLC. It is imperative that everyone know what the expectations are, and has the opportunity to participate in this high-yield strategy for success. Previously explained, the *E* and the *R* are important additions to the SMART acronym as they direct us back to the essential function of the I-PLC. That is the consistent and continuous search for both positive and negative evidence as to the impact that our instruction and students learning tactics are having on learning. The goal is to create a culture of learning.

The following is a sample of a standard short-term learning goal that was set by an I-PLC within a cycle of instruction:

> The percent of *6th Grade ELA* students at Mastery and above in *determining the central idea of a text with supporting details* will improve from *23* percent to *87* percent by *March 11th* as measured by the *Section 2, Grade 6, Formative Assessment 2.2.* The post-assessment will be given on *March 7th* with data into the I-PLC Evidence-Organizer by close of business (COB) on *March 9th.*

Notice that the last portion of the goal spells out the expectation that the post-assessment will be given in time to get the data from each PLC member into the evidence organizer for the group at least 36 hours prior to the meeting.

When setting the amount of growth expected, teams simply look back to the baseline data. The initial number of students who are at "Mastery" compose the starting point. From here, teachers consider adding the students from the "Partial Mastery" performance group to the number of students in "Mastery" to begin setting the goal. In the process of disaggregation, team members not only list the numbers of students in the performance categories, but they also list the names. The rationale is that we want to put a face to the data. For example, what if Suzy's grandmother died the week of the formative assessment? Suzy's teacher knows this, and also knows that based on Suzy's prior performance, she is likely to perform beyond mastery on this unit at the end. Therefore, based on this knowledge, even though Suzy's pre-assessment score may have placed her in the "No Mastery" group, her name is added by her teacher to the overarching SMARTER target list for mastery at the end of the unit.

Long-term and midterm goals can be more general in nature than the short-term goals that are actually driving the day-to-day actions of the I-PLC. For example, a long-term goal from the previous example might look like this:

Long-Term Goal

Will increase literacy in reading, math, and science over the next 3 years as measured by the State Assessments in Reading, Math, and Science.

Midterm Goal

We will increase the percentage of Grade 6 students scoring proficient and above in Reading on the State Assessment from 54 percent (54/100 students) to 72 percent (72/100 students) by next year.

In the short term, the targets that are set are directly related to achieving these long- and midterm goals. The short-term goals may actually be determined during Step 2 because ongoing formative assessment serves as the baseline for the continuing work of the I-PLC during the implementation of individual instructional cycles related to specific learning intentions. Periodic monitoring occurs throughout the year to ensure that the goals of the I-PLC are clear, coherent, and focused.

In addition to initial analysis of the data, we also seek in Step 1 to disaggregate the data further to determine which specific student subgroups are having the greatest obstacles to learning. It is not enough to say, "Our Grade 6 students just cannot do math!" During this process, the questions clearly asked should reflect deep inquiry into the following areas:

1. Which students? (The research will display whether there is a pattern of ethnicity, gender, grade level, age, socioeconomic status, language, disability, etc.)

2. Which math? (Operations and Algebraic Thinking, Number and Operations in Base Ten, Geometry, etc.)

3. What specific knowledge and skill associated in math? (Use parentheses, brackets, or braces in numerical expressions, and evaluate expressions with these symbols; use place value understanding to round decimals to any place; classify two-dimensional figures in a hierarchy based on properties; etc.)

Step 1 is about setting our sights on that group most in need of improvement and at the same time, on which area within the broad scope of the content area is most in need of the improvement. This allows for an evidence-based decision to be made about the focus of the content that will, in turn, make up the bulk of the meeting cycles of the classroom-level I-PLC.

Step 2: Measure Formatively

In Step 2, we have the content focus and the student focus driven by a preliminary goal developed during Step 1. We now use our I-PLCs to develop formative assessments to measure a baseline where our kids are working on the learning intentions that support attainment of the broader target curricular aim often referred to as an academic content standard. In addition, this also allows us to confirm where our students are in real time in regard to our focus area for improvement. These baseline data are then analyzed, and instructional planning done to differentiate support for three different performance groups on the formative assessment. Students are classified into one of three performance groups.

Performance Groups on the Formative Assessments for I-PLC

Mastery: Students are currently performing beyond the preset standard for proficiency, thus the selected strategies will be designed to extend their learning. This is facilitated using the CCSS because all we have to do is look to the next year academic content standard to extend the learning (Piagetian Strategy from Hattie, 2012; effect size: ES = 1.28). An example of a strategy representative of the *Piagetian Strategy* is when teachers recognize at what level students are processing information and using that information to inform instructional decisions. For example, looking back to the SOLO Taxonomy discussed earlier, students can process information at five key levels. Students might not grasp a solitary idea about the content, thus this represents the prestructural level. As students' progress on the learning continuum, they are able to grasp a single idea, thus we say that they have progressed to the unistructural (one idea) level. Students who deeply grasp multiple ideas in relation to the targeted learning intention then represent a higher level of processing, thus signifying progress into the multistructural level. When students are able to relate ideas and describe relationships, such as cause and effect, then we recognize that they have reached the relational level. Last, when students are able to extend the ideas beyond what is presented, such as hypothesizing and theorizing, we recognize that they have reached the extended abstract level. When teachers know at what level students are processing in regard to learning intentions, they are then able to make more informed decisions about instructional adjustments, and feedback for students.

Knowing the level of processing is essential for a teacher's ability to provide the appropriate level of feedback for students progressing with learning. The message from Hattie (2012) is clear: "we must know what students already know, know how they think, and then aim to then progress all students towards the success criteria of the lesson" (p. 42). This message expands with the concept of applying pressure to accelerate to higher levels of understanding to achieve growth to those students who are already proficient. We can also look to the SOLO taxonomy to help take the intended responses of students to the next level.

Partial Mastery: These students are currently not proficient, but based on the evidence collected from the formative assessment task, the consensus is that they will master the learning intention after targeted instruction. Students may be showing some mastery of the surface-level intentions, but processing at the intended deeper levels of the success criteria is not evident.

No Mastery: These students currently are exhibiting no mastery of the surface or deep aspects of the intended learning intentions represented by the success criteria, and based on the assessment-elicited evidence collected from the formative assessment task, the consensus is that they will require intensive targeted instructional support to eliminate their hypothesized obstacles to learning. Intensive scaffolding of previous years learning may be necessary to extend student knowledge and ability to the current year's learning intentions derived from the academic content standard.

An I-PLC sets the criteria for each of the three performance groups prior to the administration of any pre- or post-assessment. Therefore, when scheduling the baseline assessment, this assessment should be given at least 7 days or so before the unit actually begins in order to allow the I-PLC to come back together to complete the process of formative analysis before instruction on the learning intention. That is, the team uses the baseline data to identify the learning needs of the students, levels of processing (surface or deep), and then selects the teaching strategies directly designed to eliminate those identified obstacles to learning and/or extend learning to students already at mastery on the knowledge and skills under consideration in the current unit (content focus of between 2–6 weeks) of instruction.

Figure 7.4   Sample of Pre-Unit Assessment Evidence

Target Curricular Aim: *Determine a central idea of a text and analyze its development over the course of the text, including how it emerges and is shaped and refined by specific details; provide an objective summary of the text.* (CCSS ELA, RI.9–10.2, p. 40)

Learning Intention: *Determine a central idea of a text and analyze its development over the course of the text, including how it emerges and is shaped and refined by specific details.*

Success Criteria:
1. Identify key details within an informational text.
2. Combine the key details of an informational text and determine the central idea.
3. Justify the selection of the central idea based on specific textual details from the text.

Teacher	# Tested	# Mastery	% Mastery	# Partial Mastery	# Partial Mastery	% No Mastery	No Mastery
Rose	57	12 Janice, Lucy, Hap …	21%	35	25 Bo, Suzy, Jill …	43.8%	10 Liz, Bob, Greg …
Mayan	42	10 Julio, Kim, Candy …	23.8%	32	28 John, Luke, Mark …	76.1%	4 Dale, Dennis, Robin, Kate …
Dan	50	7 Lisle, Javon, Lamont …	14%	43	32 Lavon, Jermicia, Otis …	86%	11 Tim, Charles, Matt …
Kristin	70	18 Kendall, Leroy, Tyrone …	25.7%	52	35 Tim, Peyton, John …	50%	17 James, Andy, Clifton …
Total	219	47 Janice …	21.4%	172	120 Bo …	54.7%	42 Liz …

A major key to the success of the next step, Step 3 is that members of the team organize and disaggregate their data. As team members proceed through the steps of the process, remember that the more detail given at the student level to the separation into component parts of the evidence, the more likely that student needs will be more closely identified at the micro level required to help determine what the student needs to do next to progress in their learning.

Team members should be clear about which learning intention the assessment is addressing and also what will be the performance group classifications before giving the assessment. If using similar cut points to those in Figure 7.4, then teachers can simply label folders as "Mastery," "Partial Mastery," and "No Mastery" when scoring formative tasks and pre- and post-unit assessments. Subsequently, as teachers score the assessments they place the students' papers into the corresponding folders. This helps facilitate the formative analysis of the evidence that is accomplished in Step 3.

Ideally, team members have this evidence compiled at the individual classroom level, and then forward these data to the member on the team responsible for helping to compile and organize the data. Just as is true of any good collaborative structure, I-PLCs function best when there is a division of labor and engagement by all team members through the designation of roles. As individual team members, one of the process norms for this team learning is that data is sent to the "Evidence Organizer" at a predetermined time prior to the meeting. This Evidence Organizer then compiles the evidence for the entire team (as seen in Figure 7.4) using a simple spreadsheet. This stage saves a great deal of time in Step 3 of the process of I-PLC.

Step 3: Analyze for Evidence

Once we have the baseline evidence, we again repeat Step 1 by drilling down into that data to determine individual student strengths and obstacles. We also disaggregate this analysis as we group strengths and obstacles into the three performance groups of Mastery, Partial Mastery, and No Mastery. What we end up with is a list of strengths and obstacles to learning for the three groups. An example is Table 7.5.

In Step 3, individuals identify the strengths and obstacles to learning, both within the various performance groups and within their student populations. When coming together with the group, this step is when the true formative analysis begins. Think of this stage as a fact-finding mission. Team members sift through the data and discuss

Table 7.5 Step 3 Template

Mastery	Strengths		Obstacles	
	Surface	Deep	Surface	Deep
Partial Mastery	Strengths		Obstacles	
	Surface	Deep	Surface	Deep
No Mastery	Strengths		Obstacles	
	Surface	Deep	Surface	Deep

common errors, trends, patterns, and obstacles to learning that appear in the various performance groups (see Figure 7.6). In addition, teachers are seeking to determine the level of processing (surface or deep) of the students when they are making errors or exhibiting strengths. Previously, we discussed the importance of teachers knowing where students are in the journey of learning. What is intended here is more than simply having the broad view at the surface content level of where students may be struggling. The analysis here is also in reference to answering the key questions (1) with what surface elements are students at mastery, (2) with what surface elements are students struggling, (3) with what deep elements are students at mastery, and (4) with what deeper elements are students struggling?

Once strengths and obstacles are identified in Step 3, team members make evidence-based inferences about the root causes and the performance processing levels (surface or deep) in regard to the various strengths and obstacles. This analysis is done for each of the identified performance levels. The research base to support this step comes most recently from John Hattie's (2012) work in *Visible Learning for Teachers* where Hattie found that the effect size for "Formative Evaluation" was very high (effect size $d = .90$, where effect size $d = .40$ is equivalent to 1 year of academic gain; Hattie, 2009). Just as Hattie found this strategy valuable for adult learning, research proves that many influences deemed important for student learning are vital for adults as well. Specific to the concept of *formative evaluation*, this author believes the converse is also true. In addition to formative evaluation, the research is very clear about the effectiveness of self-reported grades (see Hattie's [2009, 2012] work on *Self-Reported Grades, d = 1.44*) and the use of formative assessment (Black & Wiliam, 1998, 2009). This is a key step in teachers and students using formative assessment evidence to impact teaching and learning.

Figure 7.6 Sample: Nonfiction Writing Assessment—Considering Both Sides of an Argument

Strength	*Mastery*		*Obstacles*
Surface Students are able to identify key details	**Deep** Students supported claims and provided details of both sides of the argument	**Surface** Minor grammatical errors	**Deep** Students need metacognitive skill development around self-editing
Strength	*Partial Mastery*		*Obstacles*
Surface Students understand what it means to state their opinion	**Deep** In some ways, students provided details to support their opinions	**Surface** Student unable to recognize two sides to an argument separate from their own	**Deep** Students need to be able to compare and contrast an opinion and claim Students need deeper understanding of the importance of how details support claims
Strength	*No Mastery*		*Obstacles*
Surface Students are able to define their opinion	**Deep** Students have some understanding of how using organizers helps in writing	**Surface** Students were unable to state their opinion clearly	**Deep** Students did not support their claim, or the counterclaim with any detail

Not only are teams looking for obstacles to learning, but they are also looking to find strengths of the various performance groups. When looking at ongoing formative evidence, teachers assess the relative success of their strategies. This facilitates a need to not only ask "why" students are underperforming or at a less than mastery level, but just as important to ask the same question when student performance is at mastery or above, and correspondingly to investigate at the levels of student processing, surface or deep. The idea is that if we can leverage these strengths in a way that helps eliminate obstacles, we are attacking the obstacles to learning from two simultaneous positions: from a position of strength and a position of targeted improvement.

Returning back to the template from Step 3, teams continue with two more operations: to prioritize the obstacles to learning so that focus is on the most pressing needs first, and apply root cause analysis about possible reasons for student learning obstacles. Popham's (2008) definition of formative assessment is about making use of "assessment-elicited evidence" to make decisions about future and ongoing instruction; this is what formative assessment is all about. By first addressing the most pressing needs it allows us to select strategies that target eliminating student obstacles to learning, and just like any good PLC, it also addresses those students who are already at mastery by choosing a strategy to help extend their learning. This is true differentiation of instruction; this is how teachers with 35 students in a class can actually take differentiating instruction from a hope to a reality.

Teams attack obstacles in prioritized order based on the professional judgment about which of the obstacles, if eliminated, will have the greatest impact on student learning. The Focus Model also recognizes the importance of both surface-level and deeper level aspects of learning. Teams may find that for students to progress to deeper levels of understanding that they first must address deficits in surface-level aspects. This is the type of strategic thinking that is facilitated by the I-PLC process. This not only is a process steeped in inquiry, but it also is a process that honors the professional might of the teachers involved. I-PLCs are a vehicle to harness the combined power of educators by allowing them to draw on their collective wisdom and experience in solving the most pressing problems faced in the processes of teaching and learning. Thus, translating those judgments into targeted action that directly addresses varying student needs in the learning intentions.

Moving through the process, again please note that this analysis is done for all performance groups. It is important that this differentiated analysis is performed with the goal of performing a root cause analysis as close to the student level as possible. These prioritized evidence-based inferences guide the creation of action plans containing specific strategies to address the student groups' most pressing needs. It is critical that team members go beyond just the simple identification of errors in student understanding. The most powerful goal of assessment is to make valid evidence-based inferences about student learning and then develop action plans based on that understanding (Popham, 2003). Making inferences about the root causes of student errors are vital to pairing action plans with targeted instructional strategies meant to address these specific barriers to student learning.

One of the shortcomings with attempts at collaboration around data occurs when teams aimlessly move from disaggregation to the selection of strategies. It is the intentional root cause analysis and assessment elicited evidence-based inference making that powers the process of the I-PLC to make significant improvement in student achievement. This process also operationalizes the true strength of formative assessment according to the research.

Step 4: React With Strategies

From Step 3, the team has a list of prioritized obstacles to learning, or in the case of the Mastery group, those students who need their learning extended beyond proficiency. In Step 4, taking into account the evidence-supported inferences made in Step 3, which is at the heart of formative assessment, teams make instructional decisions directly aligned to targeting these obstacles to learning. Teachers are now deciding on research-based high effect size strategies to take a focused approach to addressing student needs.

Because the I-PLC process is a scientific action research-based approach to teaching and learning, we want to reproduce effective practices once we have identified those obstacle busters. Therefore, we ask teachers to be very specific about the strategies they choose. Deciding that we simply use a "graphic organizer" is not enough. I-PLCs are about creating equity across all classes for all students. In order for this to occur, then *all* students need the following: a reasonable opportunity for exposure to the same rigorous learning intentions and success criteria, and the opportunity to experience the same high effect size strategy with the greatest chance for success that represents the most probable way of engaging students with equitable teacher action, thus allowing students access to a rich and viable curriculum. Accordingly, teachers commit to using a shared strategy to extend student learning and/or eliminate obstacles to learning. Certainly teachers may have to make real-time decisions in the classroom during the heat of instruction when they enact another strategy. In his 2007 book *The Art and Science of Teaching*, Marzano called this characteristic *withitness*. It would be a shame if teachers do not implement real-time instructional strategies if the situation calls for it, but at the same time, teachers commit to using the identified strategies for the minimum amount of time as decided in Step 4.

In addition, if teachers are able to anticipate possible needs for adjustment in instruction before implementing the intended strategies, then they can extend the use of formative assessment into making these real-time instructional adjustments. In order to consider these adjustments as true formative assessment (per the definition prescribed to earlier) and not simply serendipitous adjustments to in-class monitoring, this preplanning is critical (Popham, 2008). Think of this concept as Plan A and Plan B. Teachers then preplan some type of formative assessment task, such as thumbs-up/thumbs-down, traffic signal, or other strategy to gauge real-time student understanding of the implementation of strategy A. Depending on the outcome of this previously planned formative assessment task, teachers might choose to continue with the Plan A strategy if response was "good" or revert to the Plan B strategy if results were less than stellar. The key is that for this to be truly considered formative assessment, these actions must be planned beforehand and not simply actions enacted by the teacher in the heat of the instructional battle (Popham, 2011). The template for this action might look like Table 7.7.

Here is an example of this strategy:

Based on the prioritized need of students not being able to support arguments with details from a text, *3 days per week for 15 minutes per day*, teachers will <u>illustrate or model whole group with the graphic organizer #3.1B</u> how to identify the argument in a text and then identify the details used by the author of the text by using the SMART board and <u>self-talk as the teacher uses a highlighter to identify the details</u>.

Up to this point in the I-PLC process, the conversation focused primarily on the students. With Step 4, team members begin to shift the focus to adult engagement in the form of developing action plans leading to the selection of research-based high effect size instructional strategies that are targeted to the identified needs as discussed in Step 3. Steps 3 through 5 compatibly work together to ensure that the

Table 7.7 Step 4 Template

Mastery (Green on Template)	Prioritized Strength	Evidence-Supported Inference	Adult Action		Duration	
			A	B	A	B
Partial Mastery (Yellow on Template)	Prioritized Obstacles	Evidence-Supported Inference	Adult Action		Duration	
			A	B	A	B
No Mastery (Red on Template)	Prioritized Obstacles	Evidence-Supported Inference	Adult Action		Duration	
			A	B	A	B

strategies selected are targeted to real-time needs exhibited through analysis of the most current evidence available for the students. Ideally, this analysis is ongoing and based on multiple sources of data.

This real-time application (of the evidence-based inferences to the action-oriented instructional strategies selected to address the root causes of student learning error) drives the impact potential of these strategies on student performance. The question becomes, *Currently, if the real-time selection of the instructional strategies that teachers choose to deliver content is not based on valid evidence-based inferences from assessment-elicited evidence, then what is the basis for the selection of these instructional strategies . . . assumption . . . whimsy . . . preference?* It makes sense, both intuitively and through research to base the selection of these strategies on timely formative interpretations of the students and the evidence collected from this evaluation.

Important considerations for these instructional strategies are that they are clearly articulated, not only qualitatively but also quantitatively. For example, just simply saying that teachers are going to "model" the use of a graphic organizer for students does not contain the specificity required if the hope is that all teachers are going to use the shared strategy with all classes.

The following strategy has a better chance of re-creation from class to class:

> *Teachers will <u>model by using the document camera and a highlighter with a sample piece of text</u> the use of <u>the graphic organizer 6.2</u> during <u>whole group</u> instruction for <u>15 minutes per day</u> for 3 days per week.*

The selection of a shared strategy for each performance group simply states that all teachers commit to using the advocated strategy for the minimum specified amount of time. In addition, as special circumstances arise in the classroom, this does not limit teachers from making impromptu decisions about employing strategies. This sharing of best practice by teachers strengthens the instructional climate across the entire team. The ongoing analysis of evidence from multiple sources helps identify those strategies that are having a positive impact on student learning, and modify or eliminate those strategies that are having little or adverse impact on student learning. The key is that these strategies are clearly articulated qualitatively and quantitatively so that the ability to replicate the strategies is high.

Because a strategy is chosen for each performance group, this process facilitates differentiation of instruction within the classroom. For example, if the team has disaggregated their student performance evidence into the three groups "Mastery," "Partial Mastery," and "No Mastery," then the I-PLC selects a specific strategy for each performance level group. For illustrative purposes say *Strategy 1, Strategy 2,* and *Strategy 3,* respectively. In this scenario, the Mastery group receives instruction via *Strategy 1,* while the Partial Mastery performance group receive the benefit of *Strategy 1* and *Strategy 2.* Last, the group of students in most urgent need of additional support, the No Mastery group, receives the benefit of the intervention of *Strategy 1, Strategy 2,* and *Strategy 3,* including possible intervention from outside resources available within the school.

As illustrated, the crucial nature of Step 4 necessitates that teachers use this time to react with instructional strategies most likely to address specific student needs. Because a strategy is chosen for each performance group, not only are the students in the performance groups Partial Mastery and No Mastery receiving the additional support and attention they deserve, but also those students who are already at Mastery are being targeted by a strategy aimed at stretching them beyond their current level of performance. Ideally, the I-PLC process attends to all students' learning needs, and continuously monitors the team's impact on all students. This is fundamental to the four questions that support the work of professional learning communities. Those questions are the following: (1) What do we want all students to know and be able to do? (2) How will we know if students have learned it? (3) What will we do if students have not learned it? and (4) What will we do if students already know the learning intentions?

Step 5: Test the Hypothesis

The key to Step 5 of the I-PLC process is the development of planned tasks, both formal and informal, that lead to an ability to make evidence-based decisions about whether the strategies selected in Step 4 are having the intended impact. At best, instructional decisions are an educated guess or a hypothesis. This statement is in no way meant to negate the importance of the decisions that teachers and school leaders make on a daily basis. These decisions, when well made, are based on the best evidence that educators have at the time. We see the same types of decisions made in courts of law, medical research, and in numerous other prestigious professions on a daily basis. The strength of the decision is only made more impactful by the ongoing monitoring and the use of ongoing formative assessment or testing to see if the decision was actually the "best" decision. So, once a hypothesis is formulated, the next logical step is to test that hypothesis. This is where the other uses of the I-PLC really roar into action. That is the ongoing preplanned collaborative analysis of student work, teacher peer assessment of implementation of selected high effect size instructional strategies, and the impact of these decisions on student performance regarding the learning intentions and success criteria.

The power of formative assessment relates to actually using the assessment-elicited evidence to improve instructional decision making. Therefore, one suggestion is that teachers test their instructional hypotheses, both formally and informally, at many junctures throughout the learning cycle. This is especially critical at the beginning of a learning cycle and before moving on to another learning cycle. Ideally, there is ongoing evidence collection to assist planned decisions about adjustments to instruction and to determine if learning is occurring at a rate that validates the original hypothesis regarding selected strategies. Evidence should either validate or invalidate hypotheses made about which instructional strategies are the right course of action.

Hypothetical statements, often referred to as "if . . . , then . . ." statements can be formulated to help test the efficacy of current instructional decisions. These types of statements are often referred to as *theories of action.*

Multiple sources of evidence are better for making decisions than are solitary test scores. As a result, we recommend a combination of ongoing monitoring of student work and formative assessment tasks to determine the impact of instructional strategies. Conversations within the I-PLCs of what level of evidence is needed to make adjustment decisions is critical to the success of the implementation of an effective formative assessment process. These adjustment triggers can be determined before instruction and throughout instruction to ensure that decisions are made in a timely manner with the aim of improving both teaching and learning. In addition, the "then" portion of this statement should reflect the predetermined success criteria for the particular learning intention in question. Thus, once again, hopefully the cohesive nature of TFM shines through as each foundational piece is interwoven into the fabric of this comprehensive vehicle for school reform and improvement.

Thus, this "If . . . , then . . .," statement allows I-PLCs to develop planned formative tasks to help students and teachers fill in the gaps of where the student is presently in regard to the learning intention and the desired status.

Step 6: Evaluate Implementation

Hattie (2009, 2012), Marzano (2003, 2007), and Dean, Hubbell, Pitter, and Stone (2012) have all determined that effective strategies implemented at the appropriate time and with the appropriate adaptation can have

Table 7.8   Step 5 Template

If (Adult Action):
Teachers model the identification of key details from an informational text by using a document camera, highlighter, and a sample piece of text to show the effective use of the graphic organizer 6.2 during whole group instruction for 15 minutes per day for 3 days per week.
Then (Target Student Response):
Independently, students are able to analyze a piece of informational text and identify the key details by using the graphic organizer 6.2 and a highlighter.

dramatic impact on student achievement. Hattie's (2009) research shows that many of these high effect size strategies, such as "self-reported grades (ES = 1.44)" and "Piagetian strategies (ES = 1.28)" have the potential to produce a greater positive effect on student achievement than the negative impacts associated with either "home environment (ES = 0.52)" or "socioeconomic status (ES = 0.52)."

To ensure the fidelity of the implementation of the strategies selected in Step 4 and tested in Step 5, it is incumbent on the PLC to clearly state what the expectations are for adult behavior, and then also state the success criteria (the expected student behavior if the student has mastered the learning intention) and if the adult action (instructional strategy) is having the intended impact. This allows teachers to begin with the end in mind (Wiggins & McTighe, 1998) by clearly stating up front what they expect students to be doing and saying if the strategy proves successful. In addition, to determine if the learning is approaching the appropriate level of rigor, teams also clearly articulate what the scaffolding of rigor or rigor of responses (remember SOLO taxonomy) will look like in the ever-increasing rigorous tasks students are able to complete around the concept or skill, if thinking is not only developing, but also deepening. If the strategy is having the intended outcome on the learning process, then a product of this type of strategic thinking (on the part of the I-PLC in relation to the success of the selected strategies) is most easily articulated in an expanded "if . . . , then . . ." statement. The following is an example:

Step 6 Considerations

1. What is the teacher doing and saying?

2. What is the student doing and saying?

3. At what level of the task (surface or deep) is the student able to respond?

Based on the work of City, Elmore, Fiarman, & Teital, L. (2010). *Instructional rounds in education: A network approach to improving teaching and learning.*

In addition to the many findings discussed thus far related to John Hattie's (2009) research in *Visible Learning*, one additional aspect that had a significant effect size on student achievement (effect size d = .75, where effect size d = .40 is equivalent to 1 year of academic gain) was the influence of "Teacher Clarity" (p. 126). In addition to teachers talking to other teachers about best practice, the act of teachers clarifying expectations (success criteria), learning intentions, and communication of these important aspects of the learning process to students has the power to greatly improve teachers' impact on the students they serve. Accordingly, when I-PLCs are specific and accurate in their descriptions of professional practice and the learning intentions expected as a result of the implementation of these strategies, it is more likely that these strategies can be replicated successfully from class to class. This ability to replicate success and identify specific areas of planned practice to revise, modify, and adjust are at the heart of structured effective teacher collaboration and formative assessment.

The articulations of expectations of what the intended strategy will look like if implemented with fidelity, and the intended results, or cognitive changes that we expect to see in the students participating in instruction with these strategies are what we describe as *Monitoring Windows* in the I-PLC process. *Merriam-Webster's Online Dictionary* (2013b) defines *fidelity* as "accuracy in details; exactness." As the name implies, this is precisely the clarity we seek in the "if ..., then ..." statement that is represented by the monitoring window. Because we are seeking to enunciate for each strategy, exactly what this strategy will look like, sound like, and feel like in the classroom and then exactly the change in behaviors we expect to see in students if the strategies are having the intended impact on student prioritized needs in these intention clarifying statements, we then create a monitoring window for each strategy employed. Also notice that the monitoring window is concerned with the student's level of processing, whether surface or deep, as well.

An example follows of the monitoring window for the previously articulated instructional strategy:

Instructional Strategy

Teachers will <u>model the identification of key details from an informational text by using a document camera, highlighter, and a sample piece of text</u> to show the effective use of <u>the graphic organizer 6.2</u> during <u>whole group</u> instruction for <u>15 minutes per day</u> for <u>3 days per week</u>.

James Popham's (2003) and John Hattie's (2012) work validate this search for impact in the evidence of student performance—the search makes the "covert" variables of student ability "overt" by measuring the success, or the lack thereof, of our instruction by

Table 7.9 Step 6 Monitoring Window

Instructional Strategy: Teachers model the identification of key details from an informational text by using a document camera, highlighter, and a sample piece of text to show the effective use of the graphic organizer 6.2 during whole group instruction for 15 minutes per day for 3 days per week.	
What is the teacher doing and saying? The teacher will model the use of graphic organizer 6.2 and a highlighter for the identification of key details in an informational text.	*What is the student doing and saying?* The student will use a highlighter and graphic organizer 6.2 as a tool to identify the key details in an informational text. Students should be able to discuss their justification for the selection of certain details as key to the text.
What SURFACE level aspects have students mastered? Not mastered? Example: Can students simply define a key detail? Are students able to analyze a text and identify the key details?	*What DEEP level aspects have students mastered? Not mastered?* Example: Can students go beyond simple identification and justify their choices with textual evidence?

seeking evidence from what we see the students' knowing or doing. As Hattie (2012) stated,

> The act of teaching requires deliberate intervention to ensure that there is cognitive change in the student; thus the key ingredients are being aware of the learning intentions, knowing when a student is successful in attaining those intentions . . . and knowing enough about the content . . . so that there is some sort of progressive development. (p. 16)

Any concisely written monitoring window for each performance group will attend to the prioritized learning gap, the strategy selected to react to that need, and the success criteria, the behavior we hope to see in students as a result of the implementation of the strategy, and finally, evidence in student work to support that the strategy is having the intended positive cognitive impact on student learning. "The excellent teacher must be diligent about what is working and what is not working in the classroom" (Hattie, 2012, p. 17). It is the ability to use the monitoring window to help I-PLCs make instructional adjustments and monitor impact on learning that promote this excellence in learning. Because this is such a critical part of the process, PLCs devote a substantial amount of the meeting time to developing the monitoring windows for each identified instructional strategy.

The monitoring windows represent the equity that we intend for all students because

- these measurement tools are focused on the instruction surrounding the key learning intentions,
- these learning intentions are derived directly from the target curricular aims, and
- the I-PLCs made a collective commitment that all students will master these intentions.

According to Hattie (2012), "the differences between high-effect and low-effect teachers are primarily related to the attitudes and expectations that teachers have when they decide on the key issues of teaching . . ." (p. 23). Therefore, although the strategies provide students varying routes to arrive, the ultimate goal for all students is the same—mastery of the target curricular aim.

Step 7: Reevaluate Progress on Goals

Step 7 is a critical step in the I-PLC process. Though many protocols give lip service to being driven by goals, in the I-PLC process teams are constantly evaluating the progress of the long-, mid-, and short-term goals. In Step 7, I-PLCs also revisit the short-term SMARTER goal set in Step 2, which was designed to make the midterm goal a reality.

For example, if the midterm goal initially set in Step 1 was to move from 40/100 students at Mastery to 69/100 students to Mastery by May 1, then each goal set in regard to the learning intentions should be based on that end goal of moving 69/100 students to the mastery level or above.

Because of this continuous formative search for evidence of learning and the impact of adult actions, the I-PLC process differs from many other data-driven decision-making processes that only perform assessment at the beginning and end of the instructional unit (one pre- and one post-assessment). The teams create planned assessments that occur throughout the unit in relation to the identified learning intentions, as many as twice a week or more to monitor goal attainment. This evidence is then the basis of discussion for the team to take back to Steps 3 through Step 6 of the I-PLC process to determine if strategies are having their intended impact. One of the most candid parts of this discussion must center on the evidence as to whether the strategy was actually implemented as intended. This requires outside help and support to the I-PLC through the effective input and feedback of school leadership and peers. Instructional leadership from administrators is most effective when it is helping ensure the fidelity of implementation. This is true not only with the seven-step process, but also just as importantly, when dealing with the fidelity of the implementation of the high effect size strategies identified to eliminate student obstacles to learning or to accelerate learning.

To get a picture of what the I-PLC process looks like over the course of a year, it is helpful to develop an "Impact Calendar" like the one in Table 7.10. Ideally, as reflected in the table, meetings occur weekly and are aligned to the accomplishment of long-, mid-, and short-term goals.

Table 7.10 Impact Calendar

Date	Impact-PLC (I-PLC) Actions
August 1, Thursday	*Setting Long-term Goals **Midterm Goals Choose Pre-Unit Assessment for Unit 1
August 8	Unit 1: I-PLC Pre-Unit Analysis
August 15	Collaborative Analysis of Student Work Samples Unit 1: I-PLC Formative Task Analysis for Learning Intention 1
August 22	Unit 1: I-PLC Formative Task Analysis for Learning Intention 2
August 29	Unit 1: I-PLC Post-Unit Assessment Analysis for Broad Target Aim
September 5	Summative Assessment for Unit 1 Unit 2: Pre-Unit Assessment Analysis
September 12	Lesson Study Unit 2: I-PLC Formative Task Analysis for Learning Intention 1
September 19	Unit 2: I-PLC Formative Tasks Analysis for Learning Intention 2
September 26	Unit 2: Post-Unit Assessment Analysis
October 3	Summative Assessment for Unit 2 Unit 3: Pre-Unit Assessment Analysis
October 10	Unit 3: I-PLC Formative Task Analysis for Learning Intention 1
October 17	Collaborative Analysis of Student Work Samples Unit 3: I-PLC Formative Task Analysis for Learning Intention 2

Date	*Impact-PLC (I-PLC) Actions*
October 24	Unit 3: I-PLC Post-Unit Assessment Analysis
October 31	Summative Assessment covering Units 1, 2, & 3 Unit 4: Pre-Unit Analysis **Midterm I-PLC Goal Check
November 7	Lesson Study Unit 4: I-PLC Formative Task Analysis for Learning Intention 1
November 14	Unit 4: I-PLC Formative Task Analysis for Learning Intention 2
November 21	Unit 4: I-PLC Post-Unit Assessment Analysis
November 28	Summative Assessment for Unit 4 Unit 5: Pre-Unit Assessment Analysis
December 5	Unit 5: Formative Task Analysis for Learning Intention 1
December 12	Collaborative Analysis of Student Work Samples Unit 5: I-PLC Formative Task Analysis for Learning Intention 2
December 19	Summative Assessment for Units 4 & 5 Unit 6: Pre-Unit Assessment Analysis **Midterm I-PLC Goal Check
December 26	Vacation
January 2	Vacation
January 9	Unit 6: I-PLC Formative Task Analysis for Learning Intention 1
January 16	Collaborative Analysis of Student Work Samples Unit 6: I-PLC Formative Analysis for Learning Intention 2
January 23	Unit 6: Post-Unit Analysis
January 30	Summative Assessment for Unit 6 Unit 7: Pre-Unit Assessment Analysis
February 6	Unit 7 Formative Task Analysis for Learning Intention 1
February 13	Lesson Study Unit 7: I-PLC Formative Task Analysis for Learning Intention 2
February 20	Unit 7: Post-Unit Analysis
February 27	Summative Assessment for Units 6 & 7 Unit 8: Pre-Unit Assessment Analysis **Midterm I-PLC Goal Check
March 6	Unit 8: I-PLC Formative Task Assessment for Learning Intention 1
March 13	Collaborative Analysis of Student Work Sample Unit 8: I-PLC Formative Task Analysis for Learning Intention 2

(Continued)

(Continued)

Date	Impact-PLC (I-PLC) Actions
March 20	Unit 8: Post-Unit Assessment Analysis
March 21	Summative Assessment for Unit 8 Unit 9: Pre-Unit Assessment Analysis
March 28	Unit 9: I-PLC Formative Task Analysis for Learning Intention 1
April 3	Lesson Study Unit 9: I-PLC Formative Task Analysis for Learning Intention 2
April 10	Unit 9: Post-Unit Assessment Analysis
April 17	Summative Assessment Unit 9 Unit 10: Pre-Unit Assessment Analysis
April 24	Unit 10: Formative Task Analysis
May 1	Collaborative Analysis of Student Work Samples Unit 10: I-PLC Formative Task Analysis for Learning Intention 1
May 8	Unit 10: Post-Assessment Analysis
May 15	Summative Assessment for Units 8, 9, & 10 (Remediation planning for those not yet proficient)
May 22	**I-PLC Meeting around Midterm Goals
May 29	*I-PLC Meeting around Long-Term Goals
June 5	I-PLC Preplanning for Next Year

The key to the success of this approach is that it takes a systematic way of setting long-term, midterm, and short-term goals and allows the I-PLC to monitor and evaluate the attainment of these goals throughout the year. The power does not simply rest in the setting of the goals, it is the actions motivated by the evidence-based decision making because of the goals that allow teams to target adult actions (strategies) to student learning needs.

Research from Harvard University also supports the need for such a systematic process like TFM to help guide schools in using data more effectively.

Boudett, City, and Murnane (2006) stated, "We have found that organizing the work of instructional improvement around a process that has specific, manageable steps helps educators build confidence and skill in using data" (p. 1). Researchers found that in addition to having a systematic stepwise process that helps educators add intention to their interactions with evidence, it is also important that this process is cyclical. That is, the last step of the inquiry process leads right back to the first step as a continuous, ongoing process. In the words of the Harvard researchers,

> Initially, schools *prepare* for the work by establishing a foundation for learning from student assessment results. Schools then *inquire—look* for patterns in the data that indicate shortcomings in teaching and learning—and subsequently *act* on what they learn by designing and implementing instructional improvements. Schools can then cycle back through inquiry and further action in a process of ongoing improvement. (Boudett et al., 2006, p. 1)

Impact–PLC Leader

At the classroom level, the facilitation of the I-PLC process is critical for the school improvement to have any sustainability and impact. Teacher leadership is essential. The role of I-PLC leader necessitates an individual who is committed to the work of ensuring that all students are successful on the targeted curricular aims. It is fundamental this person have a growth mind-set when it comes to students and staff. In addition, the team leader should be grounded in the constructions that underpin TFM; this understanding extending beyond the I-PLC process to the foundational pieces of the learning intentions, success criteria, and formative analysis.

I-PLC leaders are expected to help the team maintain focus, a collective commitment to making a connection between adult action and student results, and a commitment to acting on the assessment elicited evidence that the PLC receives as a result of actively engaging in the process. The I-PLC leader moves the work of the team to a proactive approach regarding student results and the information received from formative analysis. That is, I-PLC seeks to break the cycle of reacting to what Stephen White (2005) calls the "rear-view mirror effect" (p. 8). Many times in education, teachers inadvertently find themselves in the reactionary mode regarding data received from students who are no longer in the grade level we are seeking to improve. In I-PLC, we move beyond this reactionary scenario to using the evidence of learning in real time.

With support of the building leadership, team leaders help maintain this focus, monitor results, and deepen efficacy in the ability of individual teams to impact student achievement in a positive manner. These leaders are not expected to whip into shape wayward I-PLC members. For this cause, it is essential that site-level leaders maintain periodic conversation with the leaders of the classroom I-PLCs. Within these meetings, the administration should discuss celebrations, barriers to effectiveness, and most importantly, ways that the administration can support the work of the I-PLC. In addition to being present in the I-PLC meetings, school leaders monitor the implementation and effectiveness of the learning teams' process through the meetings with PLC leaders and the review of agendas and submitted minutes of the meetings. All this is done to support the work of the teacher-driven I-PLC and the leadership of the I-PLC.

Impact-PLC Roles

In any effective collaborative structure, there is a division of labor. Not only does this engage the various members in the commitment to the work of the group, but it also allows team members to choose to work in their area of strength. Members can be assigned various roles within the I-PLC structure. Those roles include, but are not limited to, PLC leader, notetaker, timekeeper, facilitator, evidence coordinator, researcher, communication coordinator, and so on. The following is a brief description of each vital role:

1. **PLC Leader:** Facilitates the meetings and helps maintain focus on learning by setting the agenda, helping monitor results and implementation, and maintaining efficacy in the work of the I-PLC process.

2. **Notetaker:** Records the minutes of the meetings and coordinates the communication of the minutes to all stakeholders within 36 hours before and after the meeting.

3. **Timekeeper:** Helps the PLC stay on track within the seven steps of the meeting and the minutes allotted to discussion within the agenda.

4. **Facilitator:** Helps team stay focused on the foundational pieces of TFM, specifically the learning intentions, success criteria, and effective formative assessment practices.

5. **Evidence Organizer:** Facilitates the meeting by helping to compile the data from the members of the PLC into a usable format prior to the meeting, which helps facilitate discussion around the evidence of learning.

6. **Researcher:** These PLC members research effective high effect-size instructional strategies and provide deeper insight into

possible solutions to addressing students identified needs in Step 3 of the I-PLC process.

7. **Communication Coordinator:** These PLC members maintain the evidence of team successes and help communicate to other stakeholders within the school and beyond. They help spotlight effective strategies and the impact of those strategies in helping accelerate student learning.

Each role is vital to the group, and all support the work of using the I-PLC structure to accelerate learning and celebrate the impact of effective teaching by the committed professionals within the team.

Implementation and Leadership

Sustainability of any worthwhile initiative is incumbent on the priority and support given to it by the leadership of all levels within the school. System-level, building-level, and classroom-level leadership is essential in supporting every aspect of TFM. The power of the process comes from the ability at all levels within the system to focus on a common problem-solving strategy and use a common language of improvement. Even though we may monitor different adult action points at the system level, the building level, and the classroom level, all success is measured in the form of student results. In addition to monitoring the results in the form of student outcomes, at all levels, it is important to monitor and measure implementation of the process from the top level down.

For example, at the district level, we monitor implementation of the building-level I-PLC and the impact of the level of implementation on student results. Similarly, at the building level, we monitor the implementation of the classroom I-PLC process and the impact this implementation has on student results. Additionally, implementation at the building level also involves monitoring and providing specific feedback to PLC's on selected instructional strategies. The use of monitoring windows helps school-level leaders provide accurate, timely, and specific feedback to team members regarding the practice of selected action plans. Finally, classroom-level I-PLCs monitor implementation of agreed-on strategies by looking for evidence within student work. This is accomplished by getting feedback from colleagues, and using the monitoring windows as tools to examine the real-time impact of selected strategies on student knowledge and ability to perform targeted skills in relation to learning intentions developed from the broader target curricular aims or academic content standards.

Communicating Results and Celebrating Success

Because of the powerful impact achieved by using a systematic process to address student needs in modifying and adjusting teaching and learning, it is vitally important that system-, school-, and classroom-level PLCs put thought into how they communicate these wonderful results when they are achieved. Students, parents, and community members, in addition to all stakeholders within the school, need to be given a glimpse into the power of the concerted efforts of dedicated professional educators and the impact that this effort can have on student achievement. One example in communicating these results within the school is dedicating space for teams to display their awesome results. For example, schools can dedicate a wall for teams to share the pre- and post-assessment data and the instructional strategy that lead to student results (see Figure 7.6).

In addition to Figure 7.11, teachers can include a brief narrative about the instructional action plan they used to achieve these results. The above sample is very powerful in that it belonged to a wonderfully committed educator who shared with this author (teary eyed), when this chart was placed on the I-PLC "Wall of Fame," that this was the first time in her 32 years of teaching that she had actually seen a visible representation of the impact she had on her students.

Figure 7.11

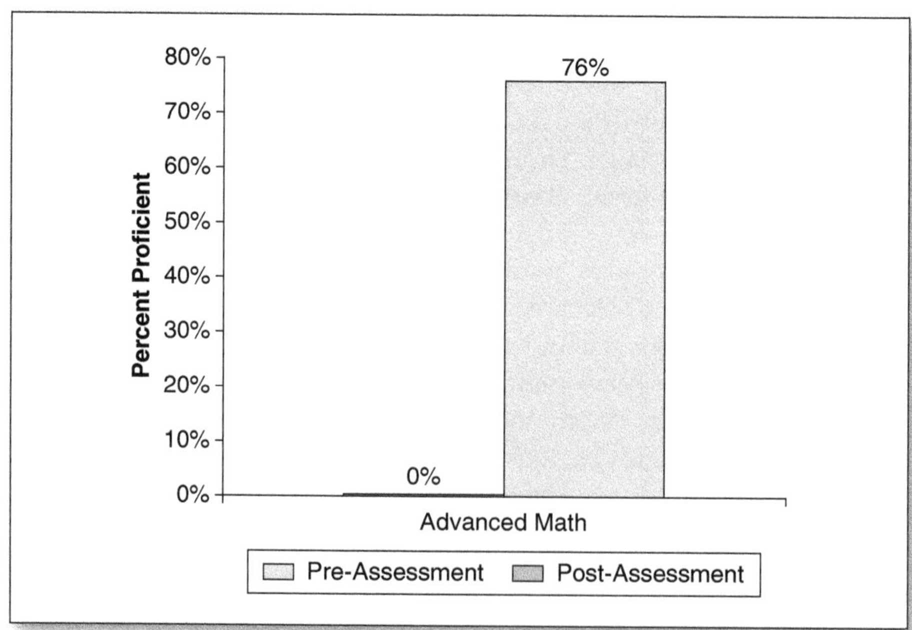

Concurrently, having students chart their individual progress is another way to engage them within the process. This gives them a visual representation of the fact that learning is about trial, effort, feedback, and learning from mistakes. As they see their individual growth, students see the powerful results of their effort on learning. School becomes not something that is simply externally done to them, but they become engaged participants within the learning process

KEY CONSIDERATIONS

The I-PLC process is the pinnacle of structured collaboration designed to improve teaching and learning. The process is systematic in that it can drive school improvement at the system, building, and classroom levels. The I-PLC process drives the work within TFM and moves professional educators from reacting to data to actually using data to be proactive and drive teaching, learning, and leadership results. Implementation of the model is critical at all levels within the system, and this implementation is facilitated by the fact that everyone within the system use similar processes, which fosters a common language of improvement. Leadership is critical at all levels within the system, and TFM, by the very nature of the process, empowers teachers at the grassroots level to take leadership within school improvement.

Guiding Questions

1. Currently, are school improvement efforts in your school or district teacher-driven? How?

2. How does your school/district use data and make connections between student results data and data on adult actions? Is that process proactive or reactive? How?

3. Does your staff perceive new initiatives as "one more thing"? Why or why not?

4. How could your school benefit from an improvement model where all pieces support one another "hand in glove"?

5. Currently, how is support inherent throughout the system (system level, building level, classroom level) so that everyone feels that each piece of the improvement process is supported and important? How could this be important?

8

A Call to Action

Action speaks louder than words, but not nearly as often.

Mark Twain

Frames of Mind

Much of the work discussed within TFM may not appear new or earth-shattering. Nevertheless, the practices described within the model framework have the power to dramatically improve teaching and learning. The problem is that teachers, principals, and central office staff must see themselves as agents of change to move this work forward from simple launch to deep implementation. This may require a change in beliefs or attitudes that some within the system have about their possible impact on student outcomes.

In *Visible Learning for Teachers*, John Hattie (2012) talks about educators needing to change their mind frame. That is, the work requires what Carol Dweck (2006) labeled the "growth-mindset," namely, the bone-deep belief that through hard work, effort, and deliberate practice, both students and teachers can deepen their understanding and learning. True, sustainable improvement outcomes will require leadership at the district, school, and classroom level to drive school improvement.

As previously stated, school improvement is not a spectator sport. The process requires learning and growth on the part of leaders, teachers, and students. TFM provides the structure to drive this learning and inquiry throughout the learning organization and the incessant motivation to connect adult actions to student results. Only when this is accomplished can the adults within schools shift from being helpless bystanders to being agents of change. TFM is the single best way to make this metamorphosis a reality.

Sense of Urgency

One of the key starting points for implementation of TFM is the creation of a sense of urgency needed to kindle such a change. Not that we wait for 100 percent buy in to initiate action, but we have to clearly articulate the rationale for the change before we can expect anyone to give the program much consideration. John Kotter (2008) wrote extensively about the need for organizations to create a true sense of urgency as the initial step to any change effort. The clear articulation of this change in the beginning can be critical in laying the groundwork for the deep implementation of any substantial shift in organizational function. Failure to create this positive momentum can be an initiative killer. Here are some brief recommendations for initiating a sense of urgency for the work in TFM:

1. Clearly articulate the empowering nature of TFM as a teacher-driven, grassroots model of school improvement.

2. At the leadership level, make the commitment to make room for the cognitive and physical work that is required to make this truly a systematic approach.

3. Build trust in the process by providing the needed support to make the process successful. The level of support should be proportional to the amount of change this action requires. *Follow through!*

4. Be visible, be engaged, and be present. This requires commitment on the part of all involved, including leadership at every level.

5. Monitor, evaluate, and give honest, accurate, timely, and specific feedback. Also, be willing to accept the same.

6. Early and often, celebrate success, celebrate success, and celebrate success.

Next Steps

What do you mean? Follow the recommendations in this book. Do not be afraid to reach outside your district or school for assistance in getting this work started and in establishing a positive support system along the way. This can help generate that sense of urgency and may help more clearly articulate the "why" as well as the "how" and the "what." Please contact this author for help in supporting your implementation of this work so that you can begin on the path of successful school improvement today.

Make It Happen

As John Hattie (2012) said, "Know thy impact, and have a *GREAT EFFECT*" (p. 192).

Appendix A
The Focus Model Curriculum Map

Units	Broad Curricular Aim (Content Standard)	Learning Intention	Success Criteria	Formative Assessment Tool	Number of Class Periods	Notes	Other
1							
2							
3							
4							
5							

(Continued)

(Continued)

Units	Broad Curricular Aim (Content Standard)	Learning Intention	Success Criteria	Formative Assessment Tool	Number of Class Periods	Notes	Other
6							
7							
8							

Appendix B
Learning Intention Progression Map

Broad Curricular Aim:

Enabling Knowledge

Enabling Sub-Skills

Appendix C
I-PLC Template

School: ____

Grade Level: ____

I-PLC Members: _____________________________________

____

____

____

PLC Leader: ____

PLC Note Taker: _____________________________________

Date:___________________ Content Area:_______________

____

Unit:___________________ Time Frame:_________________

____

Type of Meeting: ____________________________________

____

Targeted Curricular Aim (Academic Content Standards):

____

____

____

____

____

Step 1—Search the Data and Set GOALS

Long-Term Goal:

Midterm Goal:

Short-Term Goal:

Step 2—Measure Formatively

Learning Intention(s):							
Success Criteria:							
Teacher	# of Students	# at Mastery	% at Mastery	# at Partial Mastery	% at Partial Mastery	# at No Mastery	% at No Mastery
Total							

Step 3—Analyze for Evidence

Mastery Proficient and Above (Green on Template)	*Strengths*		*Obstacles*	
	Surface	Deep	Surface	Deep
Partial Mastery Not Yet Proficient (Yellow on Template)	*Strengths*		*Obstacles*	
	Surface	Deep	Surface	Deep
No Mastery Intervention Watch (Red on Template)	*Strengths*		*Obstacles*	
	Surface	Deep	Surface	Deep

Step 4—React With Strategies to Fill in Gaps or Extend Learning

Mastery	*Prioritized Strength*	*Evidence-Supported Inference*	*Adult Action*		*Duration*	
			A	B	A	B
Partial Mastery	*Prioritized Obstacles*	*Evidence-Supported Inference*	*Adult Action*		*Duration*	
			A	B	A	B

No Mastery	*Prioritized Obstacles*	*Evidence-Supported Inference*	*Adult Action*		*Duration*	
			A	B	A	B

Step 5—Test the Hypothesis

If (Adult Action):
Then (Target Student Response):

Step 6—Evaluate Implementation

Instructional Strategy:	
What is the teacher doing and saying?	What is the student doing and saying?
What SURFACE-level aspects has the student mastered? Not mastered?	What DEEP-level aspects has the student mastered? Not mastered?

<u>Step 7—Reevaluate Progress on GOALS</u>

Long-Term Goal:

Midterm Goal:

Short-Term Goal:

Notes:

References

Ainsworth, L. (2003a). *Power standards: Identifying the standards that matter most.* Englewood, CO: Lead and Learn Press.

Ainsworth, L. (2003b). *Unwrapping the standards: A simple process to make the standards manageable.* Englewood, CO: Lead and Learn Press.

Barth, R. (2006). Improving relationships inside the schoolhouse. *Educational Leadership, 63*(6), 8–13.

Berry, B., Daughtrey, A., & Wieder, A. (2009, December). *Collaboration: Closing the effective teaching gap.* Carrboro, NC: Center for Teaching Quality. Retrieved from http://teachersnetwork.org

Biggs, J. B., & Collis, K. (1982). *Evaluating the quality of learning: The SOLO taxonomy.* New York, NY: Academic Press.

Biggs, J. (n.d.). SOLO taxonomy. Hobart, TAS, Australia: John Biggs.Retrieved from http://www.johnbiggs.com.au/academic/solo-taxonomy/

Birenbaum, M., Kimron, H., Shilton, H., & Shahaf-Barzilay, R. (2010). Cycles of inquiry: Formative assessment in service of learning in classrooms and in school-based professional communities. *Studies in Educational Evaluation, 35,* 130–149.

Black, P., & Wiliam, D. (1998). *Inside the black box: Raising standards through classroom assessment.* London, England: King's College.

Black, P., & Wiliam, D. (2009). *Developing the theory of formative assessment.* Stockton, CA: Springer Science + Business Media, LLC. Retrieved from http://teacherscollegesj.edu/docs/47-Developingthetheoryofformative assessment_12262012101200.pdf

Booth, W., Colomb, G., & Williams, J. (2003). *The craft of research* (2nd ed.). Chicago, IL: University of Chicago Press.

Boudett, K., City, E., & Murnane, R. (2006, January/February). The "data wise" improvement process: Eight steps for using test data to improve teaching and learning. *Harvard Education Letter, 22*(1).

Caroll, T., Fulton, K., & Doerr, H. (2010). *Team up for 21st century teaching and learning: What research and practice reveal about professional learning.* Washington, DC: National Commission on Teaching and America's Future. Retrieved from http://nctaf.org

Chenoweth, K. (2009). *How it's being done.* Cambridge, MA: Harvard Education Press.

City, E., Elmore, R., Fiarman, S., & Teital, L. (2010). *Instructional rounds in education: A network approach to improving teaching and learning.* Cambridge, MA: Harvard Education Press.

Clarke, S. (2005). *Formative assessment in action: Weaving the elements together.* London, England: Hodder Murray.

Clay, B. (2001). *Is this a trick question? A short guide to writing effective test questions.* Topeka: Kansas Curriculum Center. Retrieved from http://www .ksde.org

Coe, R. (2002). *It's the effect size, stupid: What effect size is and why it is important.* Paper presented at the Annual Conference of the British Educational Research Association, University of Exeter, England. Retrieved from http://www.leeds.ac.uk/educol

Collins, J. (2001). *Good to great.* New York, NY: HarperCollins.

Collins, J., & Hansen, M. (2011). *Great by choice.* New York, NY: HarperCollins.

Dean, C., Hubbell, E., Pitter, H., & Stone, B. (2012). *Classroom instruction that works: Research-based strategies for increasing student achievement* (2nd ed.). Alexandria, VA: Association for Supervision and Curriculum Development.

DuFour, R., DuFour, R., & Eaker, R. (2008). *Revisiting professional learning communities at work: New insights for improving schools.* Bloomington, IN: Solution Tree.

DuFour, R., DuFour, R., Eaker, R., & Karhanek, G. (2010). *Raising the bar and closing the gap: Whatever it takes.* Bloomington, IN: Solution Tree.

Dweck, C. (2006). *Mindset: The new psychology of success.* New York, NY: Random House.

Edmonds, R. (1978). *Some schools work and more can.* [Speech at Center for Urban Studies, Harvard University, Cambridge, Massachusetts]. Retrieved from http://education-advisory.org/2007/08/effective-schools-checklist/

Elmore, R. (2002). *Bridging the gap between standards and achievement: The imperative for professional development in education.* Washington, DC: Albert Shanker Institute. Retrieved from http://nuatc.org

Elmore, R. (2006). *School reform from inside out: Policy, practice, and performance.* Boulder, CO: Westview Press.

Frisbie, D. A. (1992, Winter). The multiple true-false format: A status review. *Educational Measurement: Issues and Practice, 11*(4), 21–26.

Garrison, C., & Ehringhaus, M. (2007). *Formative and summative assessments in the classroom.* Westerville, OH: Association for Middle Level Education. Retrieved from http://www.amle.org/portals/0/pdf/articles/Formative_Assessment_Article_Aug2013.pdf

Gayle, B. M., Preiss, R. W., Burrell, N., & Allen, M. (Eds.). (2006). *Classroom communication and instructional processes: Advances through meta-analyses.* Mahwah, NJ: Erlbaum.

Giuliani, R. (2002). *Leadership.* New York, NY: Hyperion.

Gladwell, M. (2006). *The tipping point: How little things can make a big difference.* Boston, MA: Little, Brown.

Goddard, Y., & Goddard, R. D. (2007). A theoretical and empirical investigation of teacher collaboration for school improvement and student achievement in public elementary schools. *Teachers College Record, 109*(4), 877–896.

Guskey, T., Roy, P., & von Frank, V. (2014). *Reach the highest standard in professional learning: Data.* Thousand Oaks, CA: Corwin.

Haladyna, T. M., & Downing, S. M. (1989). A taxonomy of multiple-choice item-writing rules. *Applied Measurement in Education, 2*(1), 37–50. Retrieved from http://www.testing.byu.edu

Hattie, J. (2009). *Visible learning: A synthesis of over 800 meta-analyses relating to achievement.* New York, NY: Routledge.

Hattie, J. (2012). *Visible learning for teachers: Maximizing impact on learning.* New York, NY: Routledge.

Hattie, J., & Purdie, N. (1998). The Solo model: Addressing fundamental measurement issues. In B. Dart, & G. M. Boulton-Lewis (Eds.), *Teaching and learning in higher education.* Camberwell, Australia: Australian Council of Educational Research.

Hattie, J., & Yates, G. (2014). *Visible learning and the science of how we learn.* New York, NY: Routledge Press.

Iowa Department of Education. (2009). *Iowa Professional Development Model Framework.* Retrieved from https://www.educateiowa.gov/pk-12/educator-quality/iowa-profesional-development-model

Irwin, J. W., & Farr, W. (2004). Collaborative school communities that support teaching and learning. *Reading & Writing Quarterly, 20,* 343–363.

Karpinski, A. C., & D'Agostino, J. V. (2013). The role of formative assessment in student achievement. In J. Hattie & E. M. Anderson (Eds.), *International guide to student achievement* (pp. 202–204). New York, NY: Routledge.

Killion, J. (2013). *Professional learning plans: A workbook for states, districts, and schools.* Oxford, OH: Learning Forward. Retrieved from http://learningforward.org/docs/default-source/commoncore/professional-learning-plans.pdf?sfvrsn=4

Kotter, J. (2008). *A sense of urgency.* Boston, MA: Harvard Business Press.

Learning Forward. (2011). *Standards for professional learning.* Retrieved from learningforward.org/standards

Learning Forward. (2013). *Learning communities.* Retrieved from http://www.learningforward.org/standards/learning-communities#.UkyOAdIgea8

Leithwood, K., Seashore Louis, K., Anderson, S., & Wahlstrom, K. (2004). *How leadership influences student learning.* New York, NY: Wallace Foundation, the Center for Applied Research and Educational Improvement, and the Ontario Institute for Studies in Education. Retrieved from http://www.wallacefoundation.org

Leithwood, K., Seashore Louis, K., Anderson, S., & Wahlstrom, K. (2010). *Learning from leadership: Investigating the links to improved student learning.* New York, NY: Wallace Foundation, the Center for Applied Research and Educational Improvement, and the Ontario Institute for Studies in Education. Retrieved from http://www.wallacefoundation.org

Marzano, R. (2003). *What works in schools: Translating research into action.* Alexandria, VA: ASCD.

Marzano, R. (2007). *The art and science of teaching: A comprehensive framework for effective instruction.* Alexandria, VA: ASCD.

Marzano, R. (2012). Writing to learn. *Educational Leadership, 69*(5), 82–83.

Maslow, A. (1943). A theory of human motivation. *Psychological Review, 50*(4), 370–396. Retrieved from psychclassics.yorku.ca/Maslow/motivation

Maslow, A. H. (1954). *Motivation and personality.* New York, NY: Harper & Row.

Merriam-Webster Online Dictionary. (2012a). Efficacy. Retrieved from http://www.merriam-webster.com/dictionary/efficacy

Merriam-Webster Online Dictionary. (2013a). Collaboration. Retrieved from http://www.merriam-webster.com/dictionary/collaboration

Merriam-Webster Online Dictionary. (2013b). Evaluate. Retrieved from http://www.merriam-webster.com/dictionary/evaluate

Merriam-Webster Online Dictionary. (2013c). Fidelity. Retrieved from http://www.merriam-webster.com/dictionary/fidelity

Merriam-Webster Online Dictionary. (2013d). Success. Retrieved from http://www.merriam-webster.com/dictionary/success

Merriam-Webster Online Dictionary. (2014a). Ability. Retrieved from http://www.merriam-webster.com/dictionary/ability

Merriam-Webster Online Dictionary. (2014b). Criterion. Retrieved from http://www.merriam-webster.com/dictionary/criteria

Merriam-Webster Online Dictionary. (2014c). Psychomotor. Retrieved from http://www.merriam-webster.com/dictionary/psychomotor

Merriam-Webster Online Dictionary. (2014d). Teach. Retrieved from http://www.merriam-webster.com/dictionary/teach

Michigan State University. (2009). *Writing test items.* East Lansing, MI: Board of Trustees. Retrieved from http://www.scoring.msu.edu/writing-test-items.html

Mississippi State University. (2012). *Research & curriculum unit: Career pathways initiative.* Starkville, MS: Author. Retrieved from https://www.rcu.msstate.edu/MDE/PathwaystoSuccess.aspx

National Governors Association (NGA) Center for Best Practices, & the Council of Chief State School Officers (CCSSO). (2010). *Common core state standards initiative.* Washington, DC: Author. Retrieved from http://www.corestandards.org/assets/CCSSI_ELA%20Standards.pdf

Nuthall, G. (2000, Spring). The anatomy of memory in the classroom: Understanding how students acquire memory processes from classroom activities in science and social studies units. *American Education Research Journal, 37*(1), 247–304.

Oliva, P. (2009). *Developing the curriculum* (7th ed.). Boston, MA: Pearson.

Popham, W. J. (2003). *Teach better, test better.* Alexandria, VA: ASCD.

Popham, W. J. (2008). *Transformative assessment.* Alexandria, VA: ASCD.

Popham, W. J. (2011). *Transformative assessment in action: An inside look at applying the process.* Alexandria, VA: ASCD.

Popham, W. J. (2012). *Assessment bias: How to banish it.* Boston, MA: Pearson. Retrieved from http://ati.pearson.com

Popham, W. J. (2013). *Everything school leaders need to know about assessment.* Thousand Oaks, CA: Corwin.

Popham, W. J. (2014). *Classroom assessment: What teachers need to know* (7th ed.). Saddle River, NJ: Pearson.

Reeves, D. (2006). *The learning leader: How to focus school improvement for better results.* Alexandria, VA: ASCD.

Reeves, D. (2010a). The write way. *American School Board Journal, 197*(11), 46–47. Retrieved from http://www.leadandlearn.com

Reeves, D. (2010b). *Transforming professional development into student results.* Alexandria, VA: ASCD.

Reeves, D. (2011). *Finding your leadership focus: What matters most for student results.* New York, NY: Teachers College Press.

Robinson, V. (2011). *Student-centered leadership.* San Francisco, CA: Jossey-Bass.

Schlechty, P. (2005). *Creating the capacity to support innovations* (Occasional paper #2). Louisville, KY: Schlechty Center. Retrieved from http://www .mikemcmahon.info/capacity.pdf

Schmoker, M. (2011). *Focus: Elevating the essentials to radically improve student learning.* Alexandria, VA: ASCD.

Senge, P. (2000). *Schools that learn.* New York, NY: Doubleday.

Suchan. (n.d.). Define your project goals and success criteria. Microsoft. Retrieved from http://office.microsoft.com/en-us/project-help/define-your-project-goals-and-success-criteria-HA001211137.aspx?CTT=5& origin=HA001214328

Surowiecki, J. (2005). *The wisdom of crowds.* New York, NY: Anchor.

Toyota. (n.d.). Kaizen. Toyota Material Handling UK, Author. Retrieved from http://www.toyota-forklifts.co.uk/EN/company/Toyota-Production-System/Kaizen/Pages/default.aspx

Troen, V., & Boles, K. (2012). *The power of teacher teams.* Thousand Oaks, CA: Corwin.

Tuckman, B. W. (1965). Developmental sequence in small groups. *Psychological Bulletin, 63,* 384–399.

U.S. Department of Education. (2002). *The No Child Left Behind Act of 2001.* Washington, DC: Government Printing Office. Retrieved from http:// www2.ed.gov/policy/elsec/leg/esea02/index.html

U.S. Department of Education. (2013). *Race to the top.* Washington, DC: Government Printing Office. Retrieved from http://www2.ed.gov/ programs/racetothetop/index.html

Webb, N. (1997). *Criteria for alignment of expectations and assessments in mathematics and science education.* Research Monograph No. 8. Washington, DC: Council of Chief State School Officers. Retrieved from http:// facstaff.wceruw.org/normw/WEBBMonograph6criteria.pdf

White, S. (2005). *Beyond the numbers: Making data work for teachers and school leaders.* Englewood, CO: Lead and Learn Press.

White, S. (2011). *Beyond the numbers: Making data work for teachers and school leaders* (2nd ed.). Englewood, CO: Lead and Learn Press.

Wiegers, K. (2002). *Success criteria breed success.* IBM. Retrieved from http:// www.ibm.com/ developerworks/rational/library/2950.html

Wiggins, G., & McTighe, J. (1998). *Understanding by design.* Alexandria, VA: ASCD.

Wiggins, G., & McTighe, J. (2013). *Essential questions.* Alexandria, VA: ASCD.

Index

CORWIN
A SAGE Company

The Corwin logo—a raven striding across an open book—represents the union of courage and learning. Corwin is committed to improving education for all learners by publishing books and other professional development resources for those serving the field of PreK–12 education. By providing practical, hands-on materials, Corwin continues to carry out the promise of its motto: **"Helping Educators Do Their Work Better."**

Learning Forward (formerly National Staff Development Council) is an international association of learning educators committed to one purpose in K–12 education: Every educator engages in effective professional learning every day so every student achieves.

www.ingramcontent.com/pod-product-compliance
Ingram Content Group UK Ltd.
Pitfield, Milton Keynes, MK11 3LW, UK
UKHW052218050726
472866UK00007B/177